The Backpacker's Manual

The
Backpacker's
Manual

Cameron McNeish

The Oxford Illustrated Press

Printed in Hungary, 1986

ISBN 0 946609 01 2

The Oxford Illustrated Press Ltd.

Sparkford, Yeovil, Somerset, England.

Reprinted 1986.

To Gina, Gordon, and Gregor

Who keep a caged bear happy between trips...

THE BACKPACKER'S MANUAL has been
originated and produced by the following.

Editor: Turlough Johnston.

Layout: Tommy Berglund, Ulf Söderqvist.

Artwork: Tommy Berglund, Lars Jödahl, Hans
Linder, Munir Lotia, Ulf Söderqvist.

Photographs: Fjällräven (pages 35 left, 38, 83, 94 top,
95 top, 131 right, jacket; Åke Hedlund (pages 42,
63, 82–83, 87, 127, 142); Bo Hilleberg (page 95
centre); Karrimor (page 35 right); Cameron
McNeish (pages 7, 10, 15, 19, 22-23, 27, 32-33, 44,
51, 58-59, 62, 70-71, 78-79, 94 inset and bottom, 95
bottom, 110, 118, 119, 126, 130, 131 left, 134, 135,
138); Optimus (page 110-111).

Lithographics: Nils Hermansson.

The publisher would like to thank the following for
their kind help in providing information and illustration material for the book: Fjällräven, Bo Hilleberg, Karrimor, Optimus, Primus.

CONTENTS

Preface

Once, during a radio interview, I was gently accused of being a little odd. We were discussing a book I had written about backpacking, and my interviewer could not, or did not want to, see further than the potential discomforts of backpacking.

He wanted to discuss the concept of carrying a heavy rucksack up and down mountains; I wanted to discuss the feel of wind on an upturned face. He grimaced at the thought of living off freeze-dried foods; I described the simple pleasure of drinking ice-cold mountain water when thirsty. He could not understand that anyone could get pleasure from sleeping out "in the middle of nowhere". I could not understand how someone could sleep in a hotel room next to a busy highway, with glaring lights, and the solid thud-thud of some nearby discotheque slowly driving them crazy, when they could lie and listen to the all-embracing sound of intense silence under a starlit sky.

Eventually, the tack was changed and I was accused of trying to escape from reality. If reality was income tax forms, how to pay the mortgage, the eternal city-centre search for parking places, and the almost continual tap-tapping at a typewriter to earn a daily crust, then yes sir, as often as my accountant would allow, I tried to escape from it!

With just a faint glimmer of respect in the eyes of my interviewer, I was finally branded "a tough outdoorsman". Much as my ego would have liked to agree to this label, I had to unfold the truth. Marine commandos are tough; the hunters and trackers of old were tough; mountaineers, struggling with the vertical snow and ice of far-flung mountains are tough; but I couldn't describe myself as tough. The technology of latter twentieth-century manufacturing skills have, in a sense, deprived me of that accolade. Lightweight orthotic boots, waterproof and yet breathable materials, micro-weight tents, and self-inflating air mattresses allow me to indulge in the wonders of the wild and remote places without undue bodily suffering. Tough, then, is not the word I would use. Skilled, perhaps, experienced, even learned, but hardly tough.

I left that young man with his darkened room, his flashing red lights and vast control panel, and as I drove away I listened on my radio to his bantering between pop records. That was his world, unreal enough to me, and a little odd. I drove through the crowded neon-lit streets of his city, cursed at the staccato stop-go of traffic lights, and longed for the green places, far removed from the twilight world of the disc jockey, his world, as real, or as unreal, as my own.

Naturally, not everyone understands. Civilized man has come a long way in the last couple of hundred years, and what was once normal practice, is nowadays generally regarded as a little freaky. The desire to walk on one's own two legs, for recreation, is hard for the person whose sole walking experience is from his front door to his car to understand. How does one relate the well-oiled flow of mind and muscle to the average non-walker whose understanding of movement has been bred on unforgiving concrete? To many, there is little value in a holiday without discos, bars, shows, constant sunshine, and days spent languishing on a beach with a couple of hundred others. Quietness, isolation, and self-sufficiency are alien thoughts to many. The very last thing I want to do is knock discos, bars, constant sunshine, and days spent on the beach. But dare I plant a simple thought? Can it be true that the wonders of modern man—the videos, telephones, and even the space race—can limit the perspectives we have of our own natural world? Perhaps modern man has an underlying need for the older, slower times, when the natural scheme of things took precedence over new ideas? This modern man most certainly has that need. Describe this return as a tonic by all means. Describe it as escapism if you like, there are even those who would describe it as an addiction.

The marvellous thing about backpacking, be it escapism or addiction, is that no matter how hooked you become, you can often satisfy your crushing desires by small doses. A one-night sortie to a nearby hill-top can often refresh the mind and the body, and purge away a clutter of problems and thoughts that you perhaps had thought insurmountable. Out there, only the simple things are worth bothering about. Where to put the tent down, what and when to eat, whether that dark cloud on the horizon will bring rain or maybe snow, why that gaggle of high-flying geese flies in chevron formation. After a while, the obvious thoughts turn to ponderables, and then, wondrously, as though free from the clutter of everyday thoughts, the mind, loosened by the space and the solitude, swings open and out flows the pressing problems, but only now in a logical, meaningful pattern that provides answers as well as questions.

Relaxation, it has been claimed, is the way to unlock the iron doors of the mind and let the brain pour out the answers to questions that you have sought. Many business tycoons now keep antechambers next to their offices, quiet, darkened rooms with only a couch to where they can retire and relax for short spells, long enough to unleash the chain of thoughts that have been crowding their brain. The results of this practice, it is claimed, are staggering. The new world-wide breed of runners and joggers also claim to have this mental faculty. When the body starts to flow in relaxed, well-oiled efficiency, the brain pours out old questions, this time with answers.

If staggering results can be achieved in darkened antechambers and on the hard unforgiving tarmac of city streets, goodness only knows what can transpire in the beauty and solitude of the great outdoors. With a tangle of wind on an upturned face, with a rich blend of heady mountain air, with a relaxed and orderly movement amid the splendour of age-old mountains, there can be few barriers left to hinder the mind from thinking clearly.

But beware. Don't be misled into thinking that backpacking is the panacea for all the immediate problems that surround everyday living. It is, after all, only a short-term release from those problems, a chance to put them into proper perspective, and the ability to do this can only be gained by practice and time. The novice backpacker may well spend days contemplating the pain and discomfort of a blister. He or she may groan daily under the weight of an overloaded rucksack. Everyday home problems may be taken over by backpacking problems, dark thoughts of snow storms or exposure or lack of security in what seems like inhospitable surroundings. He or she may suffer, as most of us do in our early outdoors careers, from the desire to cram in as many miles and peaks as physically possible in our sojourns to the wild places, almost as a lame excuse for going there. We, as a species, are far removed from the outdoor-dwelling abilities of our forefathers. Hundreds of years of soft living have denied us the inheritance that should naturally have been ours, the ability, to use a rather over-exploited and trite phrase, to commune with nature. Walking and living in the high places, or in deserts, or by some isolated shoreline, no longer come naturally to us, and must be re-learnt. We must learn to use our legs, our lungs and our hearts again. We must learn, with the aid of modern contrivances, to navigate, to forecast the weather patterns, to find the best places to sleep at night. We must learn, almost conversely, to rid ourselves of the physical and mental shackles which luxurious living has bestowed on us. But we must not forget our twentieth-century technology. That, miraculously as it seems at times, helps us to enjoy the outdoors without pain or heartache, thus aiding us in the quest for rediscovery. To reject it would be hypocritical. Few would disagree that the little gems of twentieth-century life which find their way into our packs make our escapism so much easier.

But the essence of a successful backpacking trip is not in what we carry on our backs but in the things we see, the feelings we experience, and in the sounds we hear. The miracle gear we carry allows us to enjoy these things without any degree of masochism. But there lies another trap. The dividing line between a high-comfort level at night and a high-comfort level during the day when you have to carry the damned stuff is very tenuous indeed. Practice and experience are the masters here.

Very few people who have acquired the walking habit can limit themselves to the local park. The horizons loom, and are reached, only for more distant horizons to beckon. I can, with total recall, describe what was for me an important scene. I was young and fairly recently bitten by the walking bug. In the way of youth, I believed I was worldly wise and experienced in outdoor matters. I had enjoyed a long day knocking off some hill summits that to me, at the time, seemed remote and inaccessible. As I languished in my over-inflated pride, I saw at a distance two figures approach. I will never forget them. They were lean and burnt brown by the sun. On their backs they carried frame rucksacks, and their boots were worn and tatty. In the way of the hills, they stopped and chatted, the usual conversation of backpackers, where have you been, where are you heading, and so on. In a few short snatches of conversation, my experience until that moment was concised into what it was, no more than a dozen or so hill outings. These people, like ancient gods, had come down from the hills where they had been for two weeks, not just the hills behind us, but the hills beyond, and beyond them too. I talked briefly, in awe, and remembered the distant rolling horizons I had gazed at earlier in the day, far flung and remote. As they walked away, happy and content and wholly at ease in these vast surroundings, I clearly remember thinking to myself, I want to be one of those. The awe that I succumbed to that day still hangs in my memory, and I am aware of it as I come down from the hills and meet people who gaze at me as though I were an ancient god come newly from the wilderness. The look on their faces portrays the look that must have been written all over my youthful face, years ago as I sat on the edge of what I thought a vast wilderness. The awe, I know now, was completely unjustified. I know now that the penetration of such wilderness areas takes only some experience, some knowledge, and a desire to go there. The feelings I endured at the time were the result of a fear of the unknown, a natural trepidation of what was outside the periphery of my own experience. I know better now.

The wilderness areas are open to the backpacker, and even the novice can, after a few day-walks and a few overnight stays, begin to broach their frontiers. There are vast areas open to us, even if they are being reduced at a pace that must make us stop and think. Reports are showing that many of the world's wild places are beginning to suffer from overuse. Great bagloads of rubbish have to be helicoptered out of remote areas, rubbish that has been left by backpackers, climbers, and hikers. Trails are being battered by countless thousands of boots. What can we do about it? Every backpacker should consider himself or herself to be a guardian of the wilderness. Treat the environment as gently as possible. The camp fire is a thing loved by the traditional backpacker, but it makes too big an impact on, and can be an enormous danger to, the countryside. Avoid lighting fires, use your stove instead. It may not be as romantic, but it is faster and cleaner. Don't widen the man-hammered trails by tripping along the edges; walk in the middle. Leave no signs of your passing. Too many backpackers suffer from the wall-building syndrome – they shift boulders, leaving a pitted imprint behind, to where a new imprint can be started. This happens easily, but with some thought, it can be avoided.

"Leave only footprints, take only photographs" was a standard backpacking motto for many years, but too many backpackers have left too many footprints, so that motto should now read, "Leave nothing, take only photographs, fresh air, and memories". It is our world, the only one, so far, that we have. If we do not look after it, our children will not get the chance to.

I hope that by reading this book you may become a wiser backpacker, who will care for the environment, and that those you introduce to backpacking will also be guardians of the wilderness. Backpackers are not oddballs; they are not out to keep everything that is good about this world to themselves. By informing and educating, more and more people will begin to appreciate that the wild places are a valuable commodity, a heritage that should be endowed upon our children, and their children, to enjoy with respect and care.

Even at a young age, children can go backpacking with their parents. Small children will not be able to pack much, so the parents will have to carry most of their gear, and the day must be planned around the children, with plenty of rest stops, time out for games, and a much shorter day's hiking.

Chap. 1

WALKING

A short time ago I wrote a magazine feature about walking; not the aesthetic benefits one derives from the physical exercise point of view, but a no-nonsense practical how-to-do-it feature. I supposed it was a rather hard-nosed thing to do, tell people how they should go about something they have been doing all their lives, but it is amazing how many people rang me up to tell me that they had never really thought about the actual *technique* of walking before.

To many of us, the act of walking is as natural as breathing, and it is strange that such a simple act is quickly becoming an art, pursued by a minority. To the average citizen, walking has become virtually obsolete, a poor substitute for wheels, an activity for granola-crunching freaks and elderly people walking their dogs. Sure, we all have the inherent ability to walk, in greater or lesser degrees of efficiency. Any non-disabled person can leg it about town, but the free-moving, relaxed stride of the seasoned walker has degenerated, thanks to modern social acceptances, to an awkward mimicry of the real thing. Without doubt, this degeneration has resulted because of the prevalent social acceptance of the motor car. Everyday walking tends to become disjointed; from the front door to the garage, from car park to elevator, from elevator to desk...; the hard pavements gelatinize the cartilages, rattle and tighten up the vertebrae, and boil up the feet in a swathe of friction. Something as mundane and simple as an evening walk through darkened streets is liable to have you pinpointed as a suspected criminal, or at least an odd-ball, and it is becoming more acceptable nowadays to don a track suit and huff and puff your way around as a jogger.

In our western culture, it seems that we have lost the evolutionary gift which is, after all, the basis of all human movement. We all marvel at the walking exploits of African tribesmen, speak in awe of the apparent load-carrying expertise and the strength of Sherpas, and admire shepherds and hill farmers for their ability to walk the hills in all weathers, fair and foul. And when ordinary mortals like ourselves do happen to walk a great distance, we are quick to label them as prodigious supermen. Yet it is an ability which is inherent in all of us. If a citizen of the eighteenth or nineteenth century could be reincarnated, he or she would be astounded to see that books are now written on the techniques of walking, that people pay money to have someone instruct them in the skills of movement, and that so many people are unskilled in the simple art of walking, often being physically incapable of travelling ten miles or more under their own steam. Man's environment has changed so dramatically that the efficient walker is now quite noticeable by his absence. The efficient walker has become a rare breed.

And yet, we have not forgotten the basics. Provided we are blessed with good health we can prop ourselves up and begin actually moving in an upright position only a few months after we are born. We are still capable of movement from front door to car.... We walk when necessity demands.

A bad posture while back-packing will tire you out quickly, as it puts an unnecessary strain on your

muscles. Keep your head up and your shoulders straight. Let your arms dangle loosely and if they

swing with the rhythm of your stride, let them. Don't swing your arms as if you were in the army,

and let your legs swing from the hips, rather than kicking them out from the knees.

Once we free ourselves of the box-on-wheels, something of the old *Homo sapiens* returns and we again become *Homo ambulans*, the walking being.

It has been suggested that in an average lifetime we walk some 115,000 miles (185,000 km). That is a long way—five times round the earth, or halfway to the moon. We manage to do this without undue stress. No basic instruction is necessary, the biomechanics are inherent. The US Army, the butt of so many jokes, once prepared what was to be the definitive work on the technique of walking; how to point the toes correctly, how to swing the arms in relation to the stride, the correct biomechanical position of the left nostril.... The manual was abandoned when the troops all fell down trying to do everything as per regulations. It did not take the authorities long to discover that to remember how to walk properly, one simply goes walking.

The inability to walk long distances is mostly caused by lack of conditioning, the wrong attitudes, and mental problems. The novice becomes alarmed when he realises his heart and lungs are working overtime, and that his calves and thighs are filling up with lactic acid, making them heavy, sore, and tired. He assumes he is malfunctioning and heads back to the car, which provides him with an escape to normality.

We do not have to learn to walk from scratch, but we can do a lot to learn to become efficient at it again.

The biomechanics of walking

Walking seems such a basic and obvious action that we very rarely stop to analyse it. Perhaps we can learn to become efficient at it again by doing so. Biomechanics is the study of forces, internal and external, that act upon the human body. The elements of the walking cycle, in biomechanical terms, are known as *determinants*, and they are broken up into pelvic rotation, pelvic tilt, knee flex, foot mechanics, knee mechanics and lateral pelvic displacement. This sounds complicated wrapped up in its cold clinical jargon, but basically it is as simple as this: the heel of the leading foot touches the ground having covered a distance of roughly equal to 0.65 per cent of the length of our leg; we lean forward, displacing our centre of gravity, and the opposite leg advances forward to prevent us falling over. The pelvic cradle tilts; the knee, hip, and ankle

flexes; and the stepping foot lands on its heel; then we do it all over again.

At low speeds this is a finely relaxed movement with very little apparent energy output, but as you begin to increase the stride, or accelerate the rate at which the leg swings forward, the movement becomes more physically demanding. This is because the faster you walk, the more the rest of the body comes into play. The hips, for example, begin to swing as you reach for a longer stride. As your pace picks up, the upper part of the body will counter-rotate in an attempt to counteract the swing in your hips. Since it is almost a physical impossibility to swing the trunk from side to side for miles on end, the arms take up this task, swinging in half circles to counteract the rotation of the hips. At slow speeds this action will not be evident, but at the other extreme, watch a race walker pumping with his arms and shoulders to counterbalance the effect of massively rolling hips.

This upper-body action not only helps the rhythm and balance of walking, but it ensures multiple benefits. Not only will you gain leg strength by walking, but you will make the heart beat stronger, the lungs will begin to work more efficiently, and the biceps and stomach, chest, and shoulder muscles will all benefit from the simple act of walking, a combination of muscular activity that will help turn unwanted fat into hard muscle.

Needless to say this does not happen overnight. If I am correct in my supposition that most of us are unfamiliar with the walking habit, then a quick and sudden transition from city to the backpacking trail will only result in pain, discomfort, and a notion that this backpacking game is for masochists. An abrupt departure from desks, from behind steering wheels and from behind mugs of foaming beer into a physical world of hills, wind, hot sunshine and load carrying can have a devastating effect on the most important piece of equipment we have: our body. Hearts, lungs, and muscles appear to be reluctant to being thrust into a fight without preparation, especially the heart, so it makes sense to wean ourselves into some sort of physical shape which will allow us to use the heart, lungs, and muscles without them complaining too violently.

Train, don't strain

Strangely enough, mention conditioning to nine out of ten people and they will automatically think of running. And in almost as many cases it becomes a self-defeating exercise. For one thing, there are still those who feel embarrassed at running in public, especially if they are a bit on the cuddly side. Then there are those who will step out and proceed to bash their weak bodies over a three-mile course in an attempt to thrash them into some sort of condition. Naturally, the bodies complain, and the next several days are spent nursing sore shins, sore knees, and stiff calf muscles.

Try making your conditioning specific. That is train for walking, by walking. Even more to the point, train for walking with heavy loads by walking with heavy loads. Remember that there is a world of difference between walking with a rucksack and walking without one. Demands on muscle systems are altered in many ways.

Close study of the fibres in the body's muscles will reveal that there are two types, red and white. While every individual has two types of muscle fibre, it is interesting that the ratio of their amounts varies from person to person. The red fibres tend to be slow in contracting but can work away quite happily for long periods, while the white fibres have the ability to contract quickly and powerfully. From this we can recognize that one type of fibre, the red, acts in slow and rhythmic pursuits like walking, while the white type comes into play when we sprint, downhill ski, or run for the bus. It is the red-fibred muscles we want to develop, so there is little point in going out to run. By running we develop the white-fibred muscles, and while the added cardiovascular efficiency we gain from running will help us as we walk on the trails, it will do little to hone the red-fibred muscles which we use when simply walking. So the message is simple and clear: train for walking by walking.

Assuming that you are in reasonable physical shape, have no handicaps, and have consulted a doctor before embarking on a "get-fit-for-walking" campaign, you should be able to follow this training programme without strain. You should begin four to six weeks before your backpacking trip is due to start so that the various biochemical changes that will take place within your body's musculature can sort themselves out.

Monday: Walk 5 miles (8 km) fairly fast.
Tuesday: Walk 2 miles (3½ km) slowly.
Wednesday: Try and walk 10 miles (16 km) at whatever pace you can.
Thursday: 2 miles (3½ km) again, slowly.
Friday: 5 miles (8 km) briskly.
Take a break on Saturday and Sunday.

The fast walking will bring the pulse rate up to about 120 beats per minute and will help strengthen the heart and lungs.

The rhythm method

Virtually all the modern gurus of walking recommend a harmonious and orderly movement, a walking rhythm. Michael Sandi, an American author and backpacker, suggests, "Take strides that suit your legs and the terrain, moving at a speed which feels right for you. In less than a mile you will establish a rhythm that blends pace, stride and breathing, and shifts its inner gears with changes in the land."

Hugh Westacott, an English walker and writer, agrees. "On level ground, use your natural stride and resist any temptation to lengthen it. On a gradient, the stride should be shortened, but the legs should move at the same speed, maintaining the rhythm of walking. Perhaps the best analogy is that of a motor car driven by an engine maintaining a constant speed, with the road speed controlled by infinitely variable gearing."

Robin Adshead, in his excellent primer, *Backpacking in Britain*, suggests, "Hiking is using every ounce of energy to good advantage. The stride will settle down to a proper length in the first mile or so. The whole body will learn to swing, trunk and shoulders turning slightly on the hips as the weight of the pack moves forwards. Arms are swung actively if not vigorously in a diagonal movement, and, properly timed with each stride, will add balance and drive to the gait."

Colin Fletcher, the highly literate Welshman who has been the grandaddy of American backpacking, puts it simply, "An easy unbroken rhythm can carry you along hour after hour...."

John Hillaby, the British equivalent, walks to music. "Music stored away mentally and recalled under stress or in moments of ecstasy is a boon for those who walk alone. I have skipped along to Prokofiev's wire-thin rhythms."

Perhaps the simplest and best advice comes from Harry Roberts, erstwhile editor of "Wilderness Camping" magazine. "Take it easy. Not too easy, just easy...."

Roberts's recommendation probably best of all tells us how to achieve this intangible commodity called rhythm. By walking at our own pace, within our own limitations, we can settle our bodily movements, and our minds, to what is comfortable and enjoyable, saving energy, preserving strength, and keeping in good humour. Unfortunately, this

If you walk along at a natural, easy pace, you will soon get into a rhythm that suits you and which you can keep up for long stretches.

personal rhythm can be destroyed, or left unfound, by walking in company with others.

By adjusting to the walking speed and rhythms of others, the optimal, steady-pace, automatic pilot which keeps us going is consciously, or often subconsciously, adjusted to suit the speed of whoever happens to be in front. A wrong word at the wrong time can destroy an appreciation of a particularly appealing scene; no two walkers have the same level of physiological conditioning, a situation which invariably results in one walker hurrying to keep up, or slowing down to allow his companion to keep up, breaking that all-important rhythm. This adjustment, however minor, reduces one's own walking efficiency.

To most people though, the alternative is unacceptable. A companion is, at least, a well-tried and heartily recommended safety precaution, the finest thing you can have around if you find yourself with a cracked tibia or a sprained ankle on some far-flung mountain slope. The decision to walk alone or not must be a personal one, as only the walker himself knows how experienced or otherwise he is, and how willing he is to accept solitude. It is not everyone who enjoys being on their own, and there are many people, not only walkers, who cannot identify between solitude and loneliness.

How far and how fast?

These are questions which, in a sense, can only be answered by the individual in the light of experience. Some walkers of my acquaintance set themselves strict timetables, daily mileages which must, for the sake of continuous mental stability, be met. Timetables, as far as this backpacker is concerned, are one of the things to get away from. "Takin' it easy and takin' it slow" is a good motto for the novice to bear in mind, and a walking pace which is personally comfortable evolves very quickly with experience. A well-used rule of thumb is used by joggers as well as walkers: If you can't carry on a conversation, you're going too fast. If you walk alone you may draw some strange looks from passers-by as you experiment with this simple test, but don't let it worry you.

The actual speed at which you walk is governed by so many variables that it is virtually impossible to arrive at a set figure. Naismith's Rule, the rule of thumb for simple navigation, claims that we walk at 3 mph (5 km/h) with half-an-hour added for every 1,000 ft (300 m) that we ascend, and this is probably a fair average. But remember that it is only an average. Go into a mountain range in winter, in strong buffeting winds and knee-deep snow with a 30-lb (13.5 kg) pack on your shoulders and I will bet you anything you will not walk at the same pace you would on a straight dirt track in high summer wearing only a lightweight day-pack. You must make allowances for these external factors. I know from hard-earned experience that in fair weather, I will walk a kilometre square of the map in about thirteen minutes and that I will take an extra minute to cross each contour line in the direction of up. Most of the time these facts are completely and utterly unimportant, until you are in the position of having to navigate across a great chunk of fogged-in mountain country, then it is useful to know at exactly what time you are going to reach your destination. To this end I also know, again from hard-earned experience, that I will take 130 normal length strides per 330 ft (100 m) of fairly level countryside. So, if I am walking in a blizzard, I can tell more or less exactly just how many paces it will take me to reach a particular target. Combined with the worked-out time factor, I should not go far wrong.

Trip planning also calls for a certain knowledge of how fast you are going to travel. Theoretically, it would be nice to leave home and just wander for a weekend or a week, but in general practice, we plan our trip in advance, where we are going to camp each night, and how far we will be walking each day. There is a very simple reason for all this pre-planning. Safety dictates that we tell someone where we are going, where we will be each night, and what time we will reach home. In the event of an accident, or getting lost, then someone, somewhere, will know that we have failed to make an ETA (Estimated Time of Arrival) and call out the rescue authorities. Leave a note of your route plan with a responsible person, and tell them what time you will be back. Tell the police, National Park or Countryside Ranger, tell your folks, remembering that your very life could depend on the reliability of the person you tell. Once you have committed yourself to an ETA, make absolutely certain that you meet it, and don't, for goodness sake, jump into your car, or onto the train, and shoot off home

without confirming your arrival. Time after time, mountain rescue teams find themselves scouring the hills for folk who are comfortably ensconced in a hotel somewhere, or maybe even tucked cosily in bed at home.

REST STOPS

If you need rest stops, then take rest stops. Nobody is going to give you a prize for finishing the day without having taken a break. I do not usually stop much during the day, apart from when a particular view stops me dead in my tracks, or when something or someone demands to be photographed, or perhaps when I feel the urge to stop for a while and think. If the day is wet and overcast then I

Rest stops are a necessary and pleasurable part of hiking. Sit down warmly and comfortably, take a cup of tea or coffee, and relax.

will usually tramp happily on, deep and comfortable in the depths of my waterproofs, oblivious to what is happening outside. Backpacking is such a contemplative pastime, that quite often the hours just pass like the blink of an eye. One of the silliest rules I have heard is the one about taking a ten-minute break every hour. If you need to have that sort of regime then perhaps I could, with all respect, suggest that you are in the wrong game. If you begin to feel unduly tired or puffed or bored or hungry, then why wait until your watch dictates to you the time to stop. You are free out there. Throw the shackles off and relax.

Uphills and down

A good sense of balance is important to good walking technique. Watch two laden backpackers cross a steep slope. The good walker is the one who dislodges the least stones. Your body should be poised and relaxed in such a way that when you put your feet down on the ground, it should be with a precision something akin to daintiness. Watch a party of inexperienced walkers climbing a steep hill. After they have gone, take a look at the route they have taken and you will see that it has suffered a lot more erosion than if a party of good walkers had climbed it. Toes will have been kicked into the slope rather than the foot having been placed down. The kicking will have dislodged stones, and they in turn will have rolled down the hill, possibly dislodging others. In short, bad walking technique causes erosion, as well as using up a far greater energy output.

Climbing a gentle slope generally means nothing more than a slight shortening of the stride, and leaning slightly forward, but as the mountain slope steepens you begin to step up rather than stride. Stepping up is a quick and even placing of the foot, followed by the placing of the other foot higher up the slope. You search with your eyes for footholds rather than put your foot down where it drops, and you may even find yourself using your hands as well as your feet. But even when negotiating slopes like this, it still pays dividends to try and keep up the old rhythm. Keep the pulse alive, try and move harmoniously and lightly, however laborious it may feel. There is little doubt that climbing uphill is harder than walking on level terrain. It is sweatier, makes you breathe harder, and hurts the legs more, but think of keeping the rhythm working in a lower gear; keep the continuity of the rhythm working.

As any falling rock will tell you, downhill travel is

a lot simpler than uphill. And yet, many walkers complain loudest when their knees, ankles, and thighs come under unfamiliar pressure when descending. Take it easy. Semi-running, ever popular with the flushes of youth and the ultra fit, may well jar the spine, knees, and ankles. Try allowing the legs to bend slightly at the knee, soaking up the jarring as a shock absorber would. Think of the legs as giant coil springs....

Apply a conscious effort to maintaining rhythm when walking up and down hills, and when the going on the flat becomes particularly rough. Deep sand, mud, bogs, and tall grass all contribute to a deep sense of frustration, and that frustration stems from a disruption of an even stride. Think hard about rhythm, shorten the stride to compensate for the roughness of the terrain, and try and stay light of foot. Prolonged sidehill work can strain the foot, ankle, and knee, and here the new generation of lightweight boots come into their own. The lack of ankle stricture allows you to walk along the sidehill with the foot placed flat on the slope, just as you would walk when wearing crampons, or in the same way, if you like, as fell runners negotiate sideslopes. If you are wearing the traditional, heavy leather boots, then you do not have this freedom of ankle movement, and you must edge with the inside sole of the downhill boot, a technique which not only puts a lot of strain on the leg and foot, but also puts a lot of ecological strain on the slope.

Remember: light is right

When we think of backpacking we tend to think of feet and legs, and maybe, as the name suggests, our backs. We rarely think of our arms, stomachs, or chests. And yet, according to physiologists, all these appendages are brought into useful action when we walk. What is more important is that the greater the load we carry, the more these limbs and organs are used, and the harder they work. When you put a loaded rucksack on your back, you subconsciously lean forward in an attempt to keep your centre of gravity over your legs. This is when the other muscles are brought into play. The heavier the load, the further forward you have to bend, and before long the back muscles are brought into play, striving to take some of the pressure off the legs. The moral is simple. The heavier the load, the more pressure is put on the bodily muscles as well as on the legs which have to cart it all around.

Two Israeli researchers, Schoenfeld and Shapiro, published a paper in the *Journal of Sports Medicine*, which attempted to isolate the effects of load carrying on average walkers. Several young men were asked to walk for 12 miles (20 km), under identical conditions, carrying loads of 44, 55, and 66 lb (20, 25, and 30 kg). The object of the test was to try and ascertain the maximum load a young man in good condition could carry for 12 miles (20 km), walking at a speed of 3-4 mph (5–6 km/h), without significantly affecting oxygen uptake, causing muscle damage, or showing an excessive increase in heart rate.

Previous research had shown that a walking speed of 3 mph (5 km/h) was average for most walkers, and that study's conclusion reckoned that the most efficient backpackable load equalled about forty per cent of the walker's bodyweight. The two Israelis, however, really put themselves out on a limb by claiming that the "maximum back load for long distance by an individual in good physical condition in field situations should not be more than 55 lb (25 kilograms)". So there you have it with authority. Having said all that, a back load of 33 lb (15 kg) will be a lot more comfortable, and this writer can see little reason why backpackers should have to carry much more than that in summer conditions.

Backpacking: the inner game

Someone once observed that the mind flits from thought to thought as aimlessly as a butterfly, which is all very well, but you can, with practice, make your mind *work* for you.

Jim Peters, the marathon runner of the 1960s, once said that during the most difficult part of a marathon run, when he was really suffering, he would cast his mind back to his garden in England and relive happy thoughts. This effectively took his mind from the pain of the run and by disconnecting his mind from physical discomfort, allowed his muscles to relax and perform more efficiently.

A self-induced Alpha state positively affects blood pressure and pulse rate, and there is no reason

Hiking downhill may be easier than uphill work, but don't rush it, especially if the terrain is stony. And don't let your pace pick up to the extent that you cannot stop. Let your ankles and knees flex to absorb shocks.

why it should not make walking easier and more efficient. Many sportsmen now follow the teachings and doctrines of Zen, yoga, or transcendental meditation, so can backpackers gain from tuning in to their own consciousness? The simple act of walking, especially on one's own, may well be enough to induce this Alpha state, and if the personality of the walker is receptive enough, he or she will enjoy the contemplative nature of walking without even trying. Some walkers cogitate on the happenings of the day, while others may think of loved ones at home. Some may successfully work out long-standing problems, while others enjoy less mundane thoughts. Whatever your thoughts are, discipline yourself to tune out the negative thoughts, the pain of the long uphills for example, and think pleasant thoughts. Take your mind off to a sundrenched beach somewhere; recall a particularly happy event in your life. This mental activity takes practice and discipline, but it pays quick rewards, and the nice thing is, you tend to dwell only on positive things. The hiking trails and paths of our countryside should not be for problems, unless of course your newly acquired skills of meditation allow you to work them out positively.

Sometimes, of course, certain types of walking require all the attention you can muster. Concentrate hard then, and tune in to the task in hand to the omission of everything else; but as soon as you get the chance, let your mind wander.

Whatever type of backpacker you are, you will only succeed in improving your own level of performance by getting out there. Collect your gear and go walk. That really is what it is all about.

Chap. 2

WALKING EQUIPMENT

When we set out and leave the city behind, we are in effect exposing ourselves to whatever the weather chooses to throw at us. We must therefore create our own personal micro-climate, by wearing garments which will keep us cool in hot weather, and comfortably warm in the cold. Let's start with the feet.

Footwear

It has often been claimed that a pound on the foot is equal to five on the back, a claim not based perhaps on cold clinical data, but spawned by the uncomfortable realisms of experience. As such, it tends to bear more credence among walkers and backpackers than any pure scientific analysis.

For years, blisters and how to treat them have been an unfortunate part and parcel of our outdoor activities. Whether it be the breaking in of new boots, or socks which rub the wrong way, or wearing boots which are too rigid for the activity for which they were designed, it seems that the vast majority of us accept this painful situation as an occupational hazard. On a 90-mile (160 km) backpacking trip in southern France a few years ago, when roasting hot temperatures baked the trails hard, our little group of six walkers shared the staggering total of seventy-odd blisters. I was lucky, being fortunate enough to own naturally hard feet, but there was little doubt that for several of our group, the trip became a painful memory of staggering and lurching along on red-hot feet, longing for the next stream for a cooling soak and momentary relief. One of our group, his feet more damaged than the rest, gathered us around him one night as he ceremoniously burned his boots, a pair of traditional leather hiking boots. He happily continued the walk in a pair of running-shoes and firmly announced at the end of the walk that his days

of walking in heavy boots were well and truly over. It was running-shoes for backpacking for him from then on. Now it would be foolish to claim that ordinary leather boots mean only discomfort, but for years we have simply accepted that this type of boot is the only one we should choose for backpacking. This dogmatic approach has been encouraged by outdoor centres, authors of how-to-do-it books, and various rescue authorities by their "thou shalt wear stout boots" syndrome.

But attitudes are changing. People are now admitting that heavy hiking boots are a pain: they are expensive; for the first few trips, until they are broken in, they can be uncomfortable and cause blisters; they tear up fragile ground; and they are often only worn to help nurture a "macho" image, the rambler's attempt at identification with the mountaineering heroes of the day. Thankfully, we are now reaching a stage where we have an alternative, and even more important, the new attitude amongst the majority of wilderness commentators is that most of us are overbooted for maintaining a decent comfort level, and an acceptable ecological one.

This phenomenon runs concurrently with the explosion of running-shoe manufacture. Running-shoes have metamorphosed beyond description during the 1970s. The science of podiatry, new manufacturing methods, and new materials have been combined in the production of new high-tech running-shoes that are lighter and stronger than their predecessors, offering built-in shock absorbers, heel counters, and special waffle soles. More and more people began wearing their comfortable running-shoes instead of the traditional boots on backpacking trails and realised the added freedom of being lightly and comfortably shod. In 1978, the American K.2 expedition wore Nike LDV running-shoes on all but the worst terrain of the

padded ankle cuff

shallow tread on sole

EVA midsole

orthotic footbed

Choose comfortable foot-wear that suits the walking conditions.

(Upper left) Trail shoes are really souped-up running-shoes, designed for day trips in dry climates, or for those who want to go lightweight. The nylon uppers on this type of shoe are normally reinforced with leather or suede patches, and the sole is usually tougher than that of a normal running-shoe. If you are used to running on rough surfaces, and have strong ankles and good balance, then you will probably like trail shoes, even in fairly rigorous conditons.

(Upper middle) The approach boot differs from trail shoes in having higher ankle cuffs, a greater degree of padding, superior support, and better water-proofing qualities. Approach boots are ideal for summer backpacking, being lightweight and comfortable, yet having a good deal of foot support, due to the stiff heel counters. Nylon or cordura, with leather or suede reinforcement patches, are still the most usual materials. Gore-Tex inner linings are often used to increase waterproofing. Backpackers who tend to suffer from footache, or who dislike damp feet intensely, may find approach boots just too lightweight and porous.

(Upper right) The trekking boot tends to follow the traditional walking-boot rather than the running-shoe. It tends to be heavier than the trail shoe or the approach boot. Many trekking boots attempt to blend the high-technology and high-performance characteristics of running-shoes with the padding, lateral stability, and water repellency of traditional boots. Many even succeed. One must, however, question the value of buying synthetic trekking boots that are as heavy as traditional leather boots. If I were unhappy about wearing approach boots in summer conditions, then I would simply plump for well-proven, traditional, lightweight, leather boots.

(Lower left) Construction and materials of a modern lightweight walking-boot. Most new hiking boots have EVA soles and orthotic-type Frelin-foam insoles that can be removed from the boot. Some manufacturers call these insoles "footbeds". EVA stands for ethyl vinyl acetate, and Frelin is the name of a cross-linked polyethylene fibre. When combined in the midsole in a sandwich of varying densities, EVA improves cushioning and stability. The job of the Frelin footbed is to perform a similar function in the insole—moulding itself to the shape of the walker's foot.

Most of the new boots made today are synthetic, although there are a few lightweight leather boots and suede boots. Cordura and heavy-gauge nylon are materials that are used normally with leather or suede reinforcement patches, usually sewn around the shoe where the uppers meet the sole. Soles are available in a variety of designs, the traditional Vibram sole being still much in evidence. But even Vibram soles come in a variety of patterns, some of which have very shallow treads, or lug, which will cause less damage to the ground.

In all soles, traction is important. Some boots have bevelled heels, and this allows the heels to strike the ground natural-ly, thus contributing signi-ficantly to a comfortable gait.

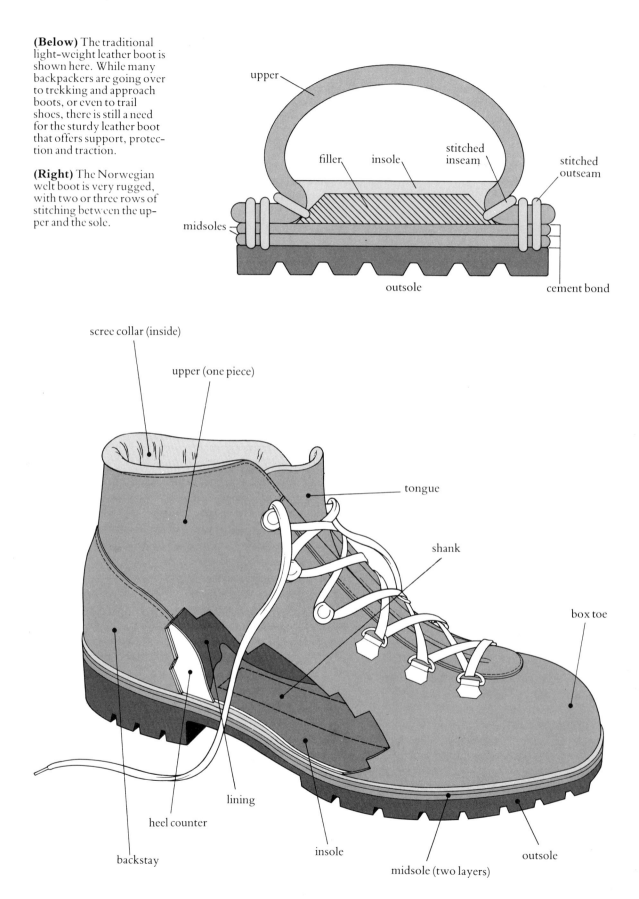

(Below) The traditional light-weight leather boot is shown here. While many backpackers are going over to trekking and approach boots, or even to trail shoes, there is still a need for the sturdy leather boot that offers support, protection and traction.

(Right) The Norwegian welt boot is very rugged, with two or three rows of stitching between the upper and the sole.

upper

filler

insole

stitched inseam

stitched outseam

midsoles

outsole

cement bond

scree collar (inside)

upper (one piece)

tongue

shank

box toe

heel counter

lining

backstay

insole

midsole (two layers)

outsole

approach march, and Reinhold Messner shocked the traditionalists by announcing that he had climbed to 26,000 ft (8,000 m) on Mount Everest during his solo oxygenless ascent, wearing running-shoes, a sure indication that the popularity of this type of footwear was about to signal a new trend towards change.

Needless to say, the running-shoe manufacturers were quick to seize on this new market, and their brief very quickly became apparent: to revolutionize hiking-boots. The result? Synthetic walking-boots made to suit a variety of differing terrains from easy rambling to hard scrambling on the mountains.

TRADITIONAL BOOTS

However we look at it, it is clear that backpacking boots as we have known them are undergoing radical changes. Increased technology, a renewed comfort-awareness by backpackers, and an increased concern about reducing environmental impact to a minimum are fast rendering medium-weight and heavyweight mountain boots obsolete. Even the specialist mountaineer is now changing his footwear to more lightweight plastic boots. But in winter time, when the snow is on the ground and you find yourself in the position of having to wear crampons to negotiate steep icy slopes, then it is a confidence boost to have your feet encased in a pair of sturdy leather boots with normal Vibram soles.

Good-quality leather boots, large enough to be worn with two pairs of socks and still allow the toes to wriggle, are still, I believe, a must for winter backpacking above the snow line. Top-grain leather has a natural resistance to water and is easily waterproofed. A minimum of seams is important, as seams are a prime source of water ingress. A good overlapping closure and a sewn-in tongue are also important in keeping water out. Obviously, the more waterproof the boots are, the greater the risk is that condensation will dampen your feet, but this is where good socks come into their own. More of that later, though.

LOOKING AFTER YOUR BOOTS

Lightweight synthetic boots need as much care and attention as traditional leather boots, and you can even increase the waterproof qualities of your lightweights by treating them regularly with waterproofing and conditioning products. Sno-Seal, Texnik, G-Wax, and Leath-R-Seal water-proofing agents are probably the best of the bunch. Particular care and attention should be given to the

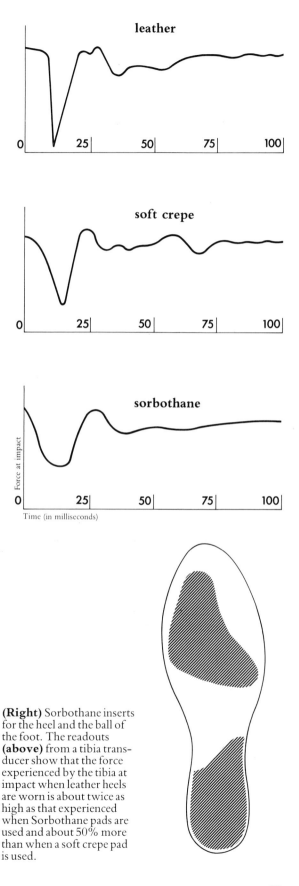

(**Right**) Sorbothane inserts for the heel and the ball of the foot. The readouts (**above**) from a tibia transducer show that the force experienced by the tibia at impact when leather heels are worn is about twice as high as that experienced when Sorbothane pads are used and about 50% more than when a soft crepe pad is used.

seams. For maximum waterproofing, treat the *insides* of the boots, too. When the boots are dirty, wash them under a tap with cold water and use a small brush to remove all particles of dirt and grit. Then, before drying, wax the boots thoroughly with one of the agents I have mentioned. As the boots dry in a warm, well-ventilated place, the waterproofing agent will dry into the seams. Once they are thoroughly dry, treat them again.

Leather boots need more care and attention than synthetic boots and should be well oiled with an oil- or vegetable-based product such as mink oil before being worn for the first time. Once the boots are treated, take them for three or four easy day trips to initiate the breaking-in process. This breaking-in process should be subtle and gradual as it takes time for the leather to warm up and for the fibres and inner sole to mould to the hiker's foot.

SOCKS AND INSOLES

Despite the various makes and types of socks available nowadays, good-quality wool socks take some beating. Wool is resilient, absorbs sweat well, and will keep the feet reasonably warm, even when it is wet. This is because the hairy surface of the wool traps the air, even when wet. Dry wool has a wicking (sweat-absorbing) action, which allows perspiration and humidity to be transported away from the skin, leaving a reasonably dry inner surface. A pair of thick wool socks with a thinner wool sock underneath is a good combination. I personally prefer two pairs of socks when I am backpacking, particularly when I wear leather boots, as two pairs tend to reduce friction and so help stop blisters forming. I usually carry a couple of extra pairs on backpacking trips, and change them round every day. Changing socks from the left foot to the right foot halfway through the day has much the same effect as putting on a new pair. Always keep your socks as clean as possible, as dirty socks insulate poorly, absorb less sweat, and increase the possibility of blisters.

Plastic inner soles or neoprene liners also help increase insulation. When you are standing still, your body weight compresses the socks, more or less eliminating any insulation value they may have had. Cold quickly seeps through the highly conductive sole of your boot and before you know what is happening, your toes are nipping from the cold. Insoles go a long way to prevent this from happening, by trapping the all-important layers of still air. Latticed pattern insoles are particularly effective.

Another form of insole that has attracted a large following in recent years is the orthotic footbed. These are shaped to the contours of your feet and often have inserts of material such as Sorbothane under the ball of the foot and under the heel. Sorbothane is a unique plastic which absorbs shock better than any known substance, and has been shown to reduce greatly the shock experienced by the lower leg during the simple act of walking. Sorbothane displaces its mass under shock, i.e. when your foot lands on the ground. As your foot rises from the ground, the Sorbothane reforms, and this cuts out any back pressure on your heel.

GAITERS

As further protection against wet feet, a good pair of gaiters should be worn when plodding through deep snow, long grass, or when the weather is wet. Gaiters fill the space between the top of the boot and the bottom of the breeches, or the area of your trousers between ankle and knee, and will prevent your lower trousers or socks from becoming wet. They also repel wind and provide an extra layer of insulation.

Clothing

In a perfect world we would not have to bother. Nakedness, though extremely practical in a Utopian dream, is, in a still calvinist world apart from such exotic spots as St. Tropez or parts of the Californian coast, disdained in the extreme, and the thousands of foregoing generations that have, from modesty, covered their bodies have robbed us of layers of insulating fats that we and our descendants might have enjoyed. Now and again though, when the rare combination of privacy and weather permit, there is an intrinsic and elemental freedom to be found in casting off our clothes and walking as God made us. That combination, however, is an unlikely one for most of us, and even if we did strike lucky with the weather and the solitude, modesty would have us peeping over our shoulder every two minutes to check that we were, in fact, alone in our nakedness.

Low-level, fair-weather backpacking means the minimum of clothing—the "bare" demands of modesty. A pair of shorts and a T-shirt are usually all that is required. Percy Cerutty, coach and mentor of the great Australian runner, Herb Elliot, used to encourage his athletes to run without the support of jockey briefs or "jock-straps", believing

(Above) Gaiters have come a long way since ancient Norwegian skiers wrapped birch bark round their lower legs to keep warm in winter. These insulated gaiters keep your lower legs warm and the snow out of your boots.

High technology has found its way into the world of lower extremities, and some modern gaiters not only protect the lower leg, but the boot as well.

(Above left) Overboot gaiters which come with or without Thinsulate insulation, and a thick rubber band forms a tight seal round the welt of the boot. The boot uppers are thus protected from nicks and scuffing. A full-length zip down the front allows the gaiters to be opened for ventilation.

(Left) Ordinary hiking gaiters, which are tied under the instep by a cord or strap. They can be bought in duck canvas, nylon, Gore-Tex, or Cordura.

that this added to freedom of movement, and the lack of infringement around the hips certainly gives an element of free movement, but again, it all depends on the individual's modesty.

Generally speaking, thoughts on clothing are linked inextricably with the weather; in winter we wear more and carry more than we do in summer. The secret is always to wear the minimum necessary for protection and comfort. Ultimately, we aim to keep the body's inner-core temperature stable by protecting ourselves from wet and cold, bearing in mind that wet and cold are not produced solely by the elements, but also by the amount of perspiration that we produce as we walk. It makes sense to put on some warmer clothing when we stop for lunch, or for extended breaks, otherwise the body moistures that we have produced will cool down and chill the body. Consideration of this theory brings us to the types of clothing we can buy nowadays. Cotton, for example, holds the body moisture and can easily chill us, while technological wonder materials like polypropylene allow the moisture to be forced outwards by the heat of the body, so keeping the inner layer of clothing dry, and therefore warm.

The purpose of clothing is twofold. In summer it protects us from the harmful rays of the sun, which will burn the skin if we are exposed to it for too long. In winter clothing forms insulating layers which trap the warmed air from the body and stop it from being carried away by simple convection. Additionally, we wear a third layer in wet weather, which enables the insulating layers to stay dry and working. This then, in theory, is the layer concept of dressing.

THE LAYER SYSTEM

Starting from the innermost layer and moving outwards, we have first the vapour-transmission layer, then the insulating layer, and finally the protective layer.

Vapour-transmission layer

Even in summer, this layer can be important. Its job is to transmit moisture quickly and effectively without losing its own insulative capabilities. Until very recently, wool was the material beloved of outdoors folk, and indeed, it is still very popular, but it has two major drawbacks. Many people find it uncomfortable to wear next to the skin. It scratches, it itches, and it needs a lot of care. In addition, after a while's wear it becomes damp and clammy, and that is exactly what we are trying to avoid. Then along came fishnet underwear. These unlikely looking garments are made up of holes, lots of them, tied together with string or cotton or, in some cases, nylon. The holes, strangely enough, are what keep you warm, or cool, whatever you want. When worn under another insulating layer, the holes allow the air to be kept in place, and so become warmed by body heat, a highly efficient insulation. When you become too warm, you simply open up your clothing and allow this warmed air to escape; simple and effective. Fishnet also keeps moisture absorption to the minimum, and if it does become wet, it dries out very quickly indeed.

Fishnet underwear has largely been made redundant though, by the introduction of "technology clothing", the polypropylenes and olefins of the underwear world. These magic materials are the lightest of all textile fibres, which makes them additionally attractive to backpackers, are comfortable to wear next to the skin, and most important of all, wick away moisture better than wool or fishnet. This lack of moisture absorption makes the modern materials useful in summer when worn by themselves. They do not become damp and clammy, and are light enough to be cool. Under another layer, they remain warm and dry at all times.

Insulating layer

We can now consider the second layer, the one which keeps you warm. Depending on the circumstances at the time, this layer may simply be a wool shirt, a turtleneck sweater, a down shirt, a number of sweaters and a shirt, or even all these plus a down-, Quallofil-, or Thinsulate-filled jacket. You can even wear a jacket of horseblankets, it does not really matter what it is, provided it forms an insulating layer or layers to swathe your body in a still, warm cloud of air. What material you use depends on a number of factors: weight, bulk, wetness of the environment, how much money you are willing to spend, and to a certain extent, fashion.

Generally speaking, most backpackers will wear a pair of wool or nylon trousers or breeches, topped by a wool shirt, and a wool sweater. In colder weather, they may exchange the trousers for insulated salopettes, or pile salopettes; they may then add some sweaters or use a fibre-pile sweater. On a recent winter trip in Norway, when day temperatures did not rise much above −10°F (−23.3°C), I wore, on top of a suit of polypropylene underwear, Thinsulate filled trousers, a wool shirt, a fibre-pile jacket with a full-length zipper down the front, and a down-filled jacket with a hood. On the ascents, when I became too warm, I took off the down jacket and unzipped the fibre-pile sweater, just enough to keep cool. When we stopped for lunch breaks, I immediately put on the down jacket again, to keep warm.

The introduction of Thinsulate and Sontique insulation, the warmth-without-bulk concept, is, in my opinion, a great advance in backpacking clothing, as it allows you to wear very warm garments underneath wet-weather jackets, which make up our next layer of the system.

Protective layer

This outermost layer protects the insulation layer from rain and snow, and from the warmth-robbing effects of wind. The configuration of this layer will again depend on several circumstances but will usually be decided by finance and the weather conditions you are likely to come across on your expedition. In effect, though, your choice of material for this outer layer will be much simpler. PTFE, or if you want the technical term, poly-tetrafluoroethylene, is the present state-of-the-art in protective materials, and will probably be more familiar in its trade names of Gore-Tex, Klimate, et al. PTFE is a laminate which allows water vapour to pass through from the inside out, and yet does not allow water in the form of rain droplets etc. in from the outside. It represents the greatest breakthrough in backpacking since the rucksack was invented. At long last, we have garments which are waterproof and, at the same time, do not cause internal condensation.

In the past, we have used a number of materials, mostly proofed nylon, for protection from the rain and snow. But when the body warmed up and began to exude water vapour as we sweated and toiled our way along the trails, the effect was very similar to that of a kettle boiling against a cold kitchen window. In no time at all, the inside of the garment would be running with condensation, soaking our insulation layers. Not so PTFE. With this material, the water vapour is passed out through the miniscule pores in the laminate by the force of our body warmth, and condensation is minimal. Because these pores are four hundred times smaller than a water droplet, rain cannot enter from the outside.

Gore-Tex, along with the other equivalent waterproof/breathable laminates, is expensive, but it works infinitely better than anything else, so is well worth the financial outlay. You can buy Gore-Tex in almost every imaginable form

nowadays: in boots, tents, gaiters, mitts, hats, and socks. It is, simply, excellent and has made the walker's and camper's life easier.

Clothing considerations

In the past ten years, there has been a considerable revolution in the manufacture of outdoor clothing. It is nowadays the norm for backpackers to be clad from head to toe in synthetic fabrics, from polypropylene underwear to fibre-pile jackets and trousers to Gore-Tex covered Thinsulate jackets. The new materials not only work better than their natural descendants but are invariably lighter in weight, easier to look after, more compact and longer lasting. They are also much more expensive than natural-fibre materials (with the exception of natural down, which is still the finest and the most expensive insulator yet conceived).

Although a book such as this dwells on equipment in large chunks, we must always remember that gear is merely a means to an end, and although many of us fall into the gear-freak category, the real reason for donning the stuff and carrying the rest on our backs is to get out there into the green and wild places of the world. The best of equipment is not a passport to these places, it merely makes life a little bit easier getting there, and when we arrive. I suspect that I derived as much pleasure from my backpacking when my protective layer was a plastic raincoat, my boots were bought second-hand from a junk shop, and my insulation-layer sweater was a paint-splattered pullover that my father had thrown out (with the arms duly cut short to fit me).

If you are completely new to backpacking, and you are not convinced that you are going to enjoy it enough, or become so involved that you are going to spend a small fortune kitting yourself out with the best, don't worry. Most households have enough bits and pieces of potential gear hanging around in attics or cupboards, just waiting to be rejuvenated into backpacking equipment. When it comes to picking out clothing, though, you should bear in mind that when cotton becomes damp, it robs the body of heat. Cotton denim jeans, therefore, are wholly unsuitable for use in damp weather, nor do they provide sufficient insulation in the cold.

Comfort and protection, rather than appearance, are the keynotes of functional outdoor clothing. If we do not feel comfortable day after day, it will not be long before discontent rears its ugly head, and we

Summer layering
When backpacking in really warm weather, wear the minimum of clothing **(left)**. Protect yourself against the sun, though, as backpacking on sunburnt shoulders can be excruciating. In very hot weather, you should protect your head, too.

(Centre) If you feel chilly, or when you stop for lunch, slip on a wool shirt or a fibre-pile jacket.

(Right) A synthetic rainsuit protects you from the rain.

will become irritable and bad-tempered. Comfort in clothing also means light weight and adequate ventilation. The ease with which garments can be put on and taken off, especially in the limited confines of a tent or snow hole must also be borne in mind.

Protection means exactly what it says: protection from the elements. The backpacker must prevent the body from being affected by undue heat, cold, and damp, separately or in combination. Hence, the layer system. We must be able to adjust our clothing, quickly and effectively, to be in tune with the weather, and to help control our own heat output. Zippers on parkas, fibre-pile jackets and sweaters allow us to do just that, and an insulation garment and a separate rain garment are infinitely better and more adjustable than a combined insulation/waterproof jacket. Remember, adjustability is the name of the game. When you become too hot, you pull off a layer or two, and vice versa when you become cooled, you can slip on a parka, sweater, or whatever to warm up again or to keep the body temperature stable.

As I have suggested, you may not wear all the garments that I have listed, but, depending on

Winter layering
Polypropylene underwear and a balaclava of the same material under a wool balaclava form the first layer. The wool shirt of spring/autumn is reinforced by extra sweaters or a combination of sweaters and a fibre-pile or down-filled sweater or parka.

(Centre) Breeches and overboots protect the lower legs and feet, and overmitts protect the hands. When it gets really cold, an insulated parka with a covering of PTFE laminate is invaluable. An insulated hood protects your head.

(Right) Extreme-weather layering. A waterproof down or synthetic insulation-suit is worn on top of the other layers. Insulated boots, extra socks, silk innermitts, pile mitts, and waterproof overmitts are also necessary. Goggles protect the eyes against glare and driving snow.

Spring/autumn layering
Apart from on the odd days of sunshine, it is time to pull on the thermal underwear **(left)**. Polypropylene is an ideal material.

(Centre) Wool or fibre-pile shirts form a good insulating layer. An armless insulated waistcoat is an additional warmer. Knickers or trousers of wool or Helanca stretch-nylon form the insulating layer for the legs. In wet weather, or when walking through wet grass, gaiters offer good protection to the lower legs.

(Right) The protective layer is formed by a rain-suit, or, if the weather is dry, by a windproof polyester/cotton anorak (as shown) which keeps the wind out. An integral hood is indispensible.

the season, you should carry them with you. It is also important to have something to change into at night in the shelter of the tent. Winter nights, especially, are long and drawn out, and if you are going to sit around all evening in damp clothes you are asking for trouble. Fibre-pile suits, polypropylene underwear, or even track suits, all make suitable garments for lounging around in the sleeping-bag, and it is often a good idea to have a spare hat as well. Remember that the head loses a great deal of body heat, so, if you feel cold, put on a hat. You will find it makes quite a difference to the way the rest of your body feels. Whatever you decide to wear at night in your sleeping bag, do not be tempted to wear them during the day. A change into fresh dry clothing is a great morale booster at night, so don't sacrifice it for a change during the day. That especially goes for socks. Keep a clean dry pair for wearing at night, and resist the great temptation to keep them on when you dress in the morning, rather than the ones which are still damp from the previous day's outing. Yes, I know, putting on damp socks in the morning is no fun and can be a great deterrent to even getting out of the sleeping-bag, but once the damp socks are on your feet, and you are out and about, it is not so bad.

Essential accompaniments

When we walk into wild and remote places, we are, in a sense, placing ourselves at the mercy of self-help should we become lost, injured, or ill. There is little chance of a friendly passer-by, the Good Samaritan, to call a taxi to take us to hospital, and there certainly will not be a policeman standing at the corner to give us directions should we become temporarily misplaced. It makes sense then to carry along with us some more or less vital items of gear, which will help us, in the worst event, to survive. These are essential items which should be carried even on day sorties from a base camp.

1 *Extra Clothing.* Most certainly a rain suit and extra insulation in case you have to spend a night outside.

2 *Emergency shelter.* A polybag, large enough to climb inside, or even better a properly designed survival bag should be carried when you do not have your tent with you.

3 *Extra Food.* If you become lost or injured, you are likely to go hungry. Carry along some food that you dislike intensely; then you will only eat it when necessity flavours it better. I carry dates; they are high protein and I loathe them. A backpacker I know carries a packet of dehydrated dogfood...

4 *Sunglasses.* In winter you will need them to reduce the glare from snow. Remember that you can become snow blind even on overcast days. In summer, they will allow you to look without screwing up your eyes and developing a headache.

5 *Knife.* Useful for: first aid, cutting off frozen gaiter straps, opening cans when you have lost the can-opener again, whittling wood to start a small fire (in emergency situations only!).

6 *Matches or lighter.* Modern, environmentally conscious backpackers do not light fires other than in an emergency. In an emergency it can be a lifesaver. It helps to be able to start one without having to rub two Boy Scouts together.

7 *First-aid kit.* It is not only good sense to carry a fairly comprehensive but lightweight first-aid kit, but you should also know how to use it. Make sure you do; someone's life, maybe your own, may depend on it. The following items make up a minimum one-man kit: Band-Aids for minor cuts, several different sizes; gauze pads for deeper

Headwear—for situations and personalities… Backpackers wear almost as many differing types of headwear as you are likely to see in even the most bizarre Easter-bonnet parade. The general criteria for a good hat are lightness of weight, good ventilation, and adequate protection from the sun, the cold, and the wind. In rain, you will normally use the hood of your waterproof jacket or parka, but if you wear glasses, you ought to have a cap with a long peak. In winter, your headgear should keep your ears warm, too.

wounds; adhesive tape for holding bandages in place, covering blisters, etc.; salt tablets; Aspirin; a needle for removing splinters, piercing blisters, etc.; a small first-aid manual, for making sure you get it right; several bandages, including an elastic bandage and a couple of triangular bandages. I repeat: this is a minimum kit. Read as much as you can force yourself to about first aid.

8 *Flashlight*. Obvious for camp convenience, but useful as a rescue aid. International distress signal is six flashes in quick succession, repeated after a minute's interval. Alternatively, SOS is three short, three long, three short flashes, repeated after a minute's interval. Carry a spare bulb and batteries.

9 *Map and compass*.

10 *Whistle*. International distress signal is same as for torch.

The pack

Next to your boots, the pack is the item of gear which demands total love and respect. If you do not get on with your boots, they will have you crawling along in utter misery. If you do not get along with your pack, it will simply flatten you until every muscle and bone in your body creaks and groans in protest. A good, well-fitting pack, properly loaded and carried, will become a loving companion, sharing in your triumphs, and constantly reminding you of the good days in the wild and green places. A badly fitting pack, or an el cheapo, save-money-by-buying-me type pack, will fight you all the way, gradually wearing you down, until you submit in frustration and acute discomfort.

In short, a good pack is damned important.

Until fairly recently, a backpacking rucksack meant the packboard frame, a throwback to the days of Snowshoe Thompson and Trapper Nelson, somewhat akin to wearing a farmgate on your back with a bag attached to it. The pack frame as we know it is recognized as having its origins in the United States. Shortly after the war, independently of each other, Jack Albert of Camp Trails and Dick Kelty made a great step forward with the introduction of the classic contour-welded aluminium external frame.

For long-distance backpacking, for carrying extra heavy loads, and for extended trail walking, the external frame pack was a huge success, but it was noticed that the more rugged the terrain became, the more the frame pack began to develop some annoying little habits. To explain the reason for this, let us examine some of the physiological mechanics

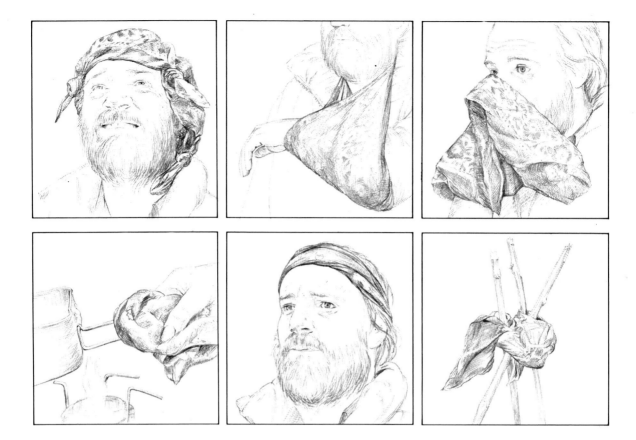

(Above) The humble bandana has many uses. See who can find the most uses for it on your next backpacking trip! Here are six to be going on with.

(Right) A typical internal-frame pack. This one has a tubular frame round the inside of the pack, fitted into a sleeve and with a frame liner in between. The tubular frame is covered with two layers of rubber foam to prevent it chafing.
(1) Frame. *(2)* Frame liner.
(3) Thick foam layer.
(4) Thin foam layer.
(5) Shoulder-blade pad.
(6) Cotton back panel.
(7) Lumbar pad. *(8)* Hip belt. *(9)* The pack's lower compartment.

(Opposite, left) An internal-frame pack, the Jaguar 4, from Karrimor, has an internal pre-shaped frame and a padded hip belt. The hips take most of the weight of this pack.

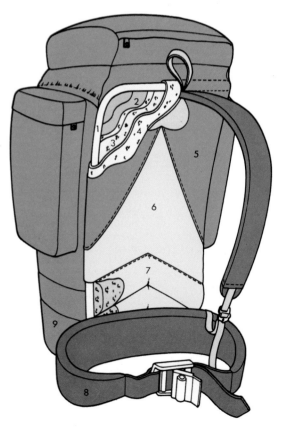

that are involved in the carrying of heavy loads.

Think of the articulation of, and the pivotal action between, the legs, the pelvis, the spine, the shoulders, and the arms when walking. With the right foot stepping forward, the right hip rotates on the lower spine, the left leg follows and immediately the left hip begins to rotate on the spine in the opposite direction. Simultaneously, the shoulders move in tandem, though diametrically opposite to the legs, and the arms are swinging back and forth to balance the stride.

On a flat trail, the rigid, back-splinting, external frame pack does not interfere with this mechanical motion, but leave the smoothness of the groomed track or trail, and head for the hills, where uneven ground, steep ground, and downhill walking cause problems in the sequence of movement.

(Right) The contour-welded aluminium frame has all the advantages of the old packboard frame and few of its disadvantages. The tubular aluminium frame is light, rigid, and remarkably strong. The two uprights of the frame follow the contours of your waist, back, and shoulders, allowing the frame to sit close to your body, bringing the centre of gravity of the load closer to that of your body. This allows the load to be carried fairly far forward, minimizing leverage against your muscles, while allowing ventilating air to flow between the pack and your back.

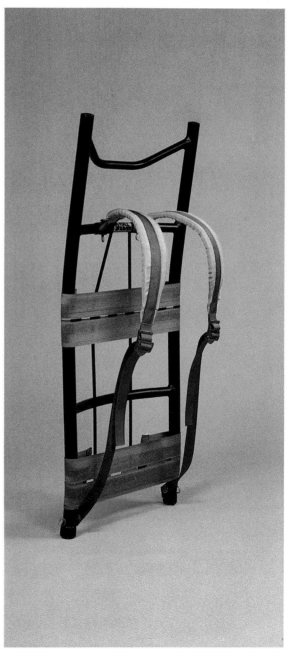

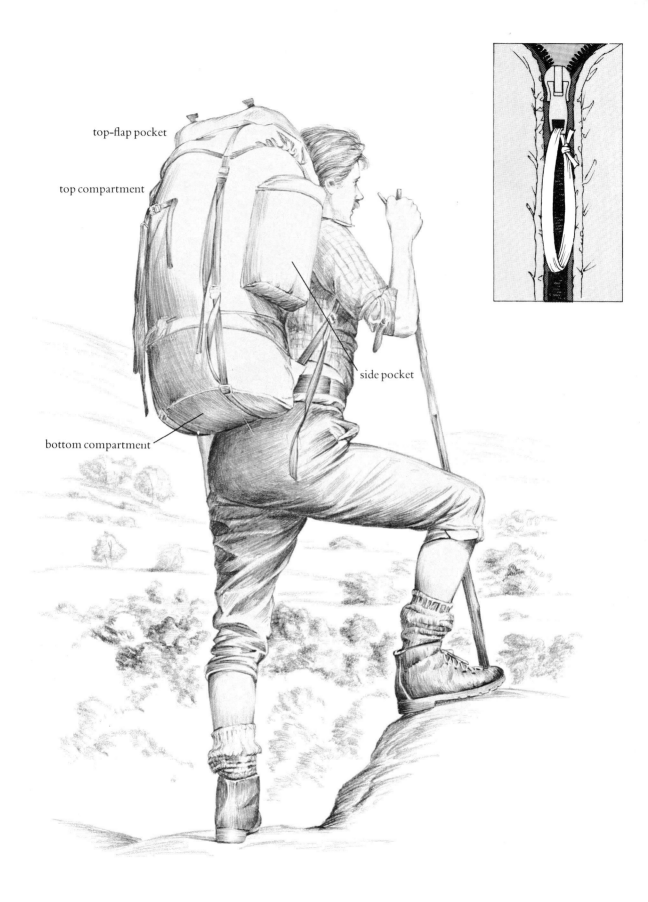

top-flap pocket

top compartment

side pocket

bottom compartment

A number of design features need to be considered when you buy a rucksack. Most backpackers seem to prefer a compartmentalized rucksack, with a divider between the top and bottom compartments. This makes packing a little bit easier. Pockets are very much a matter of personal preference, but they are extremely useful for the bits and pieces that you may be needing in the course of the day: drinks bottle, trail snacks, lunch snacks, sweater, mitts. A pocket in the top flap can hold maps, a compass, guide books, etc. Other points worth noting are quick-release toggles on the drawcord, an extension of the inner pack that covers the contents when the lid is fastened down, buckles and zippers that can be opened and closed with mitts or gloves on, and buckle straps that do not need constant re-threading.

(Inset) Tie a loop of cord to the zips on your rucksack, and it will be easier to open and close the zips when you have your mitts or gloves on.

The problem is not so much walking uphill, as the hip and leg movements are normally short, concentrated and stable, but walk downhill, and you will begin to appreciate that the hips are not only pivoting on the central axis of the spine as in normal walking, but are also tilting sideways as each leg is lowered to step down. With a rigid frame, the

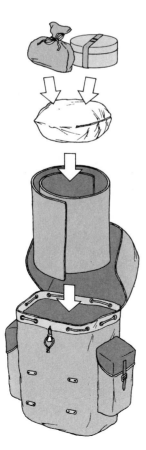

By packing your insulation pad in a coil inside your rucksack, you can protect the gear inside and you do not have the pad hanging outside, where it can get wet,

part of the frame in contact with the higher hip pushes the opposite corner of the frame off the shoulder. More serious than that, the centre of gravity of the load has shifted and is now at variance with the centre of gravity of the body, causing imbalance, which in steep, exposed ground, could be dangerous. The problem is basically one of pack sway, with the body going one way, and the pack moving the other.

Inevitably, ways were thought up of tackling this problem. By now, the hip-harness concept was being implemented in rucksack design, and this was one of the most significant steps in increasing carrying comfort. Man was never intended to be a beast of burden, and the intricate and delicate spinal column was never designed to support heavy loads. By transferring the load weight to the hips instead of the back, packs could be carried with much greater comfort and efficiency, and further, by stringing the waist-belt of the hip harness between two lower strut extensions of the frame, in effect a floating hip-belt, the body would be independent of the frame and vice versa, while still allowing the weight to be borne by the hips.

Towards the end of the 'sixties, the development of the internal frame began. It would be as well at this stage if we made the distinction between internal-frame packs and softpacks. The internal-frame pack has the frame inside a fabric envelope or sheath at the back, the soft pack has no frame at all.

Softpacks are normally used for rock climbing and are generally not considered for the loads involved in even lightweight backpacking. An exception to this rule was the Jenson pack which made a brief appearance during the early and mid-'seventies. The Jenson pack was a totally frameless design, but was so tailored, that as it was filled up with gear, it began to form its "body-hugging" shape. This was a magnificent pack, but had two real disadvantages. It could only be used with fairly lightweight loads, and you had to have the pack filled to capacity. Too little equipment inside and it hung on your back like a sack of potatoes.

Round about this time, Lowe Alpine Systems and the North Face Company began developing their own particular style of internal-frame packs. The Lowe pack had two parallel stays running up either side of the spine. The North Face had two aluminium stays crossing to form a large X. Other people were, of course, making internal-frame packs, but basically these were the two frame systems in use.

Packing a rucksack is a very individual affair, with different designs and different contents giving rise to different methods of loading. The important point to remember is to pack heavy and compact articles as close to your back as possible. When hiking, you should try to keep the centre of gravity high, but here is a tip to remember: in winter, when on ski, pack so that the centre of gravity is low, as it gives better balance.

I pack my hiking rucksack like this. *Under the top flap*: windproof jacket, shirt, things I need when I walk. *Top-flap pocket*: Guide book, note book, map, compass. *In the pack bottom*: sleeping-bag and gear, spare clothing, anything I want to keep dry. *On top next to my back*: tent, stove, and heavy foods. *On top farthest from my back*: towel, toilet bag, light food, etc. *Side pockets*: camera lenses, filters, fuel bottles, trail snacks, knife, toilet paper, matches, and anything I want ready at hand during the day. *On the outside*: insulation pad in stuff bag (unless I have packed it in a coil inside the bag).

(Below) The easiest way to put on a heavy pack is to lift it onto a rock, a fallen tree, or a bench, and then slip into the harness. Otherwise, take a firm grip on the upper part of the harness and lift the pack onto your thigh. Insert one arm through the harness strap and ease the pack up and onto your back. Insert your other arm. Bend forward and grasp the belt to fasten it. You can then, on easy terrain, slacken off the shoulder harness, allowing the hips to do all the carrying.

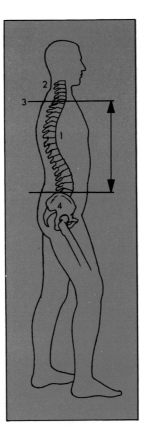

To choose a rucksack for size, put it on and fasten the hip-belt with its top edge just over your hip bone. Tighten the shoulder harness so that the frame's cross-bands fit snugly against your back and the top harness point is 2 – 3 inches (4 – 7 cm) below your high prominent neck bone. The sales person or a mirror will be needed to gauge this accurately. To obtain the correct fit, which is important for a comfortable carry, you may have to try another pack size, or adjust the position of the shoulder- and hip harnesses, if this is possible. *(1)* Spinal column. *(2)* High prominent neck bone. *(3)* Harness attachment point. *(4)* Hip bone.

The essence of good backpack design is stability and weight distribution. When a backpack is unstable, its effect can be noted in sideways sway at the shoulders. The answer to the problem lies in the correct relationship between what should be the weight-carrying medium, the frame, and the hip-belt and shoulder straps.

Basically, the difference between the two frame systems can be summed up as follows: the parallel frame is the more stable configuration but does not have the weight-distribution qualities of the X configuration, or indeed, of the old external-pack frame. Many companies now seem to solve the problem by incorporating the parallel frame in smaller packs, while using the weight-distributing qualities of the X configuration in the larger packs.

In recent years, internal-frame packs have proliferated. With all the advantages of softpacks, they nearly all now have internal frames of plastic or aluminium strips which, in most cases, can be bent to suit the shape of your own back contours. Internally framed packs usually have generous padding on the back as well, so that poorly packed gear will not cause discomfort. All the packs have integral hip harnesses, which allows the weight of the pack to be borne by the strong hip and buttock muscles rather than the shoulders.

Proper packing is essential to realize this type of pack's performance and comfort advantages. The recommended packing technique concentrates bulk low and mass (weight) high, with lateral symmetry in both bulk and mass. First of all, pack the sleeping bag. Always wrap it in a waterproof stuff sack or poly bag, as no rucksack manufactured is totally waterproof in itself. On top of the sleeping bag go other lightweight, bulky items: spare clothing, tent and food, and then the hardwear (pegs, stove, etc.) goes on the top. I normally coil an insulation pad in a tube inside the pack, and load the gear inside it. This method has two advantages. It keeps the gear inside the pack dry and protected, and it allows me to keep the insulation pad inside the bag, rather than have it hanging or dangling from the outside. If you have side pockets, they can be used for a brew kit, waterproofs, trail snacks, or camera lenses. The top flap pocket of the pack is ideal for storing maps, books, notes, sweets and chocolate.

Now that the pack is loaded up, you can gently shape the internal frame to fit the contours of your own back. This can be simply done by pressing with the knees as you pull out the top of the frame towards you. Some people like to have a space between their back and the pack so that an air flow is formed to help increase ventilation and so form a cooler carry. I personally prefer the pack as close to my body as possible, for a good body-hugging pack will give a much better carry, and if you want a big air space down the back you may as well use a frame pack. Certainly your back will sweat if the pack is pressing in to it, but my back sweats if I walk up a mountain without a pack... I am not convinced that you get sufficient air flow between your back and the pack to evaporate any condensation or sweat that forms. The bigger the space you have behind your back the more the pack will pull on your shoulders, making you lean forward to compensate. No thank you, give me a good body hugger any day, sweat and all; it will be more comfortable in the long run.

WALKING TECHNIQUES

Navigation

Navigation is the process of determining one's present position and the location of the objective, and of selecting and following the route between these two points. In its most simple form, navigation is carried out by looking and seeing, inspecting the features of the surrounding terrain, be they mountains, ridges, forests, rivers, or lakes, and then relating those features to their representations on a map. This simple technique calls for little skill, expertise being very much a function of experience. Practice is therefore vital to competent navigation.

Having said this, techniques such as taking a bearing, correcting for declination or magnetic variation, taking back-bearings, and resectioning tend to frighten the wits out of beginners, almost convincing them that, according to its nomenclature, navigation is a tricky business.

In principle, using a map and compass to find one's way in the countryside is not all that much more difficult than following a street plan in a big city. It is simply a matter of starting in the right place and in the right direction, and of always keeping a check on where you are as you continue towards your destination. Bear in mind too, that navigation is not done by map and compass alone. In good conditions, the experienced backpacker may travel for days at a time with only the occasional glance at the relevant map to check on progress and to recognize the various features he is passing. A confirmation of the lay of the land is all that is required. Nature herself is often generous in hints of direction. In northern temperate zones, the summer sun usually rises in the morning somewhere between northeast and east, is more or less due south at midday, and sets somewhere between west and northwest.

Southern hill slopes tend to be drier and sunnier than northern slopes, which are often snowier and steeper, in mountain areas usually carved and gouged into cirques by ancient glaciation. The folk who earn their daily crust by working and living in remote hill areas rarely navigate their way around their domain by map and compass. They use local knowledge based on experience perhaps going back generations, and often they have some form of built-in direction-finders in their head, a throwback to the times when men navigated purely by natural features, be they the sun, stars, or such features as I have mentioned above. You and I, in all probability, lack such inherent skills, so we are left with two choices: the use of navigational aids such as maps, compasses, and altimeters; or, we stay within the limits of our own experience by only going out in good weather conditions in areas which are familiar to us. I am sure that you will agree that the second choice is unacceptable, so we must try and develop our skills to such an extent, that we can go out in all weather conditions and find our way around quickly, competently, and safely.

MAPS

By far the most important aid to navigation is a map. The usual map for backpacking navigation is the 1:50,000, or, if you require greater detail, the 1:25,000 scale. The scale of a map can be described as the relationship between the distance on the map and the distance on the ground, therefore, on the 1:50,000 scale map, 1 inch on the map equals 50,000 inches (about four-fifths of a mile) on the ground. On a metric map of 1:50,000, 1 cm on the map equals 50,000 cm (500 m) on the ground. This information is vital when planning trips and, later, when we look at estimating time and paces.

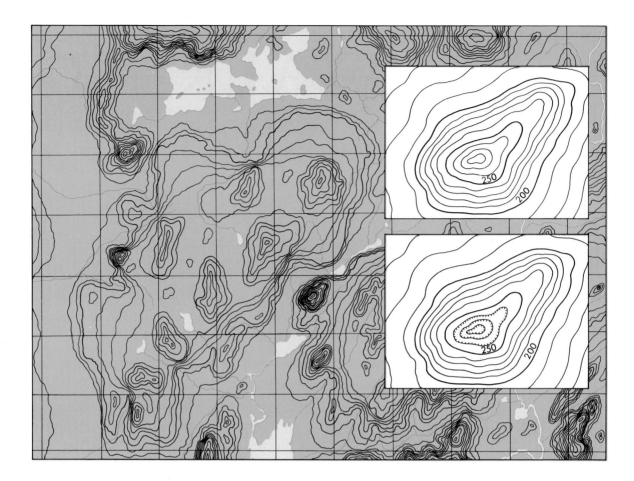

(Above) On the latest trail maps, the interval between the contour lines is 40 ft or 10 m, depending on whether the map is linear or metric. The lines all have the same colour, and every fifth line is darker. The figure against each darker line tells the height above sea level. The insets show the same contour lines, but the upper one represents a peak while the lower shows a volcanic crater.

(Left) When wilderness backpacking, an important moment during each rest stop or before starting the day's hike is to check your position on the map, so that everyone in the party knows where they are.

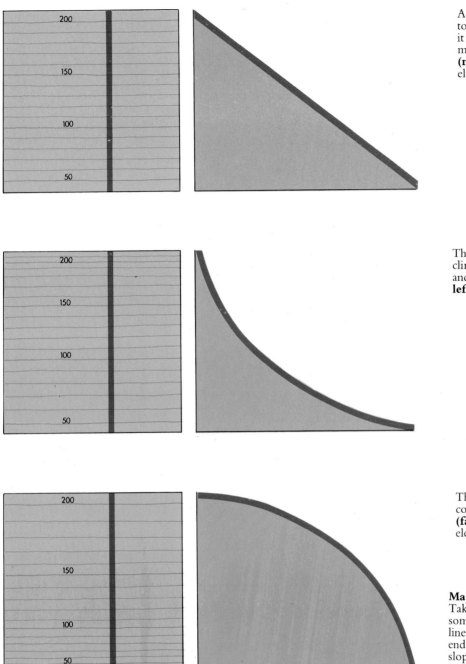

A steady climb from B to A is shown **(far left)** as it is represented by the map's contour lines, and **(near left)** in end elevation.

The dipping, or concave, climb on the map **(far left)** and in end elevation **(near left)**.

The upward curving, or convex, climb on the map **(far left)** and in end elevation **(near left)**.

Map-reading exercise
Take your map, select some areas of contour lines, and try and draw the end elevations of certain slopes on a separate piece of paper.

The natural features of the land-mountains, hills, forests, and lakes, etc.-are recorded on the map in various colours, shapes, symbols, and lines, as are various man-made features like towns, roads, paths, boundaries, and railway lines. All are explained in the key to the map, usually found in one of the corners. Symbols which depict a church with a steeple, or one without, are not of great value to backpackers, unless they have a special interest in old churches, but other symbols are of vital importance. For instance, it is important to know the map symbols for cliffs and crags, rivers and

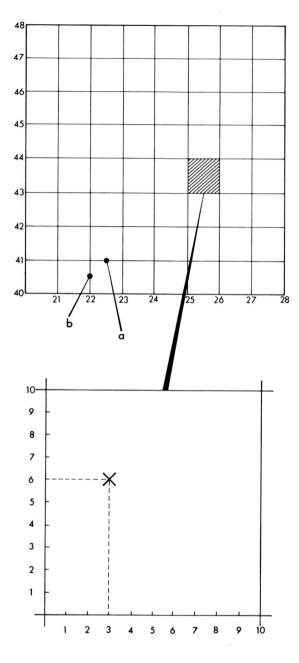

lakes, and, the most important of all, contour lines.

Contour lines on the map are lines which join points of equal height. Not only do these lines tell us the height and steepness of the land and the shape of the hills and mountains, but they tell us whether we are liable to be ascending or descending, a vital factor when working out how long it will take us to get from point *a* to point *b*.

The most important function of a map is to tell us the shape of the ground. The shape and spacings of the contour lines show the shape and steepness of the hillsides. For example, the closer the contour lines are together, the steeper the ground is. Vice versa, if the contour lines are fairly wide apart, we can tell that the ground to which they relate is not particularly steep.

Once you have mastered the art of map reading, you will be able to visualize the shape of the ground ahead of you simply by glancing at the shape and spacing of the contour lines. This is a skill which is very important indeed and can only be mastered by practice. Many people take to it quickly, while others, perhaps lacking the necessary imagination, find it ponderous and tedious. If you do not master it, you will be liable to mistake uphills for downhills, and that could lead to some rather unsavoury experiences. Look out for other clues, such as streams and rivers, which obviously cannot flow uphill, or for triangulation points or even the names of mountains which indicate the top of a hill, rather than a hollow in the ground.

Once you can tell from the map what to expect in terms of landscape, you can use this knowledge to plan your walking route. For example, if it is a very windy day, it may be uncomfortable, or even dangerous, to climb a hill by an exposed ridge. By looking at the map, you may find a valley which could offer you a safe and wind-free route almost to the top of your hill. Conversely, if it is winter, you may want to climb that ridge, rather than risk potential avalanche conditions in the steepsided valley. The contour lines on the map give you the information you require to make your intended route as safe and as comfortable as possible.

GRID LINES

The use of a grid system to simplify map reading is growing, and Britain has been leading in this field. Each map is divided into squares, the lines running north/south or east/west. Each line is numbered, and as most British maps are metric nowadays, the squares formed by the lines are 1 km², or about

Grid lines on maps help you to pinpoint your position. Read first along the horizontal lines (*a*) and you see that the shaded box (your position) lies between 43 and 44. Now go up the vertical lines (*b*) and the box lies between 25 and 26. The grid position is 4325. To be more exact, use a six-figure reference. Use the graduated side of the compass to split the side of the four-figure reference box into tenths. This gives the third and the sixth figures, and your exact position is 436253.

The best way to protect a map is to cover it with self-adhesive, transparent plastic. You can also buy an aerosol spray which "proofs" the map with a water-repellent coating.

1,190 square yards. It is surprising that other countries have not adopted this system, as the numbered lines are used for providing an exact reference to any given point on any edition of the map, i.e., you can pinpoint your position more or less exactly.

To locate a square on the map, you first look for its "easting" number, that is the line which runs across the page from east to west. You then find the "northing", that is the line which runs from top to bottom of the page, or, from north to south.

To remember which numbers come first in your grid reference, the "easting" or the "northing", there are two phrases which help you to make it easier.
1) "Along the corridor and up the stairs", or, perhaps more significantly,
2) "Walk along the flat before you fly upwards".

To pinpoint your position more accurately, you can use a six-figure reference. You simply find the four-figure square as above, and then, using the graduated side of the compass, or even just your imagination, you split the sides of the box into tenths. This then gives the third and the sixth figures.

ORIENTING THE MAP

People have been known to wander off in the wrong direction simply because they hold the map like a book with a "top" and "bottom" instead of a North and South. The map should, of course, be held in line with the features on the ground, even if this means holding the map upside down.... Look at the features around you, that lake, or forest, or that long hump-backed hill, and compare them with their representations on the map. If they are in the wrong position, turn your map around until everything falls neatly into place. Bearing in mind that we do not have an eagle's-eye view of the terrain, this map orienting takes a little bit of practice, not to mention a clear day and a load of recognisable landmarks. Once you have the knack of it though, you should be able to walk along and read your map even if it is upside down or sideways on. If you find yourself in thick mist, however, or in the middle of a featureless plain or desert, it is time to take a look at the compass.

COMPASS

Almost every backpacker I know carries a compass, and it is surprising how few of them know how to

This picture is taken from point A on the map. Points B, C, D, E, F, and G are marked on both map and photograph. See if you can relate map to photograph.

use it in all its facets. It is also surprising how many backpackers prefer to trust their own, often quirky, sense of direction, rather than trust the compass. It seems to be a human foible to disagree with the advice offered by a mere plastic tool, and time and time again we see walkers and backpackers apparently following a compass bearing, but in reality they are physically pulling away from the bearing, following a line which is dictated by that intangible commodity, their sense of direction. If you are going to carry a compass with you, and you should at all times, learn how to use it properly, and trust it implicitly.

So what do we use a compass for, apart from finding the direction of North? Surprising to some, we can use our compass to measure distances on a map; we use it as a ruler. Once you are aware of how far you have to walk, you can make an estimate, pretty accurately with practice, of the time it will take you to get there. In bad weather conditions, fog, mist or even whiteouts, this can be extremely valuable, as you can then know if you have over-shot your destination. We also use the compass to work out grid references. Compasses fitted with a "roamer" make this exercise simplicity

itself. By finding North on the compass, we can orient our map so that the top of the map is pointing North, so that the features on the map then coincide with those on the ground.

The most common use of the compass is, of course, to work out bearings, or angles, from the map to the compass. This technique is often used in bad visibility to calculate the direction in which we want to travel. Once the bearing has been worked out, by using the compass as a protractor, we then simply follow the direction of the compass. We can also use the compass to calculate bearings from the compass to the map. There are two occasions when we may want to do this: to identify a peak or some other feature and to fix the position by resection (see page 52).

MAGNETIC VARIATIONS, OR DECLINATION

Apparently, all we have to do to "set" our map, or orient it, is to find what direction North is on our compass, and then align the map in that direction. Sadly, life is not that simple. To confuse us, there are in fact three "norths" to choose from, and the one we pick will determine just how accurate or

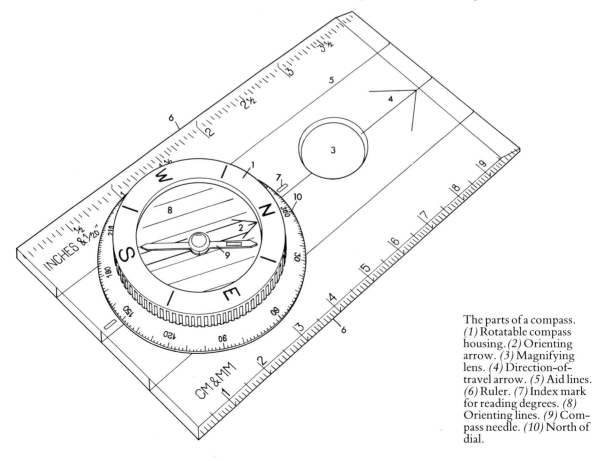

The parts of a compass. *(1)* Rotatable compass housing. *(2)* Orienting arrow. *(3)* Magnifying lens. *(4)* Direction-of-travel arrow. *(5)* Aid lines. *(6)* Ruler. *(7)* Index mark for reading degrees. *(8)* Orienting lines. *(9)* Compass needle. *(10)* North of dial.

inaccurate, our backpacking navigation is going to be.

True North is the actual North Pole, which is of no interest to us as orienteers or backpackers, unless we happen to be going there. Grid North is the North pointed at by the grid lines on the map, and Magnetic North is the north to which the compass always points and which changes slightly from year to year.

The difference between Grid and Magnetic North is called magnetic variation, or declination. The cause of this apparent anomaly is that the magnetic pull actually comes from a small island some distance west of the true North Pole, so, depending on where we are, the magnetic variation will be slightly different. A key on your map will tell you more or less what this is worth within the boundaries of the map.

True North lies in the direction of the geographic North Pole, and maps always show true North, while compass needles always point to magnetic North, about 1,400 miles (2,250 km) away. The difference between True and Magnetic North is called declination, or variation. In the Dakotas, there is very little declination, because magnetic North lies due north of them. In California, magnetic North lies a bit to the east of true North, while in New England, it is a bit to the west.

Setting the map

In Britain, the magnetic variation is usually about 8 degrees, since Magnetic North usually hovers around 8 degrees to the west of Grid North. (The magnetic variation is always to be found printed on the map.)

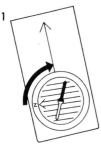

1

(Above) To set declination on your compass and to orient your map, you read first what the declination is on the declination key on your map (in this example, it is 352 degrees).
1 Then turn the compass housing until N points in the same direction as the direction-of-travel line.
2 Place the edge of the compass parallel to any meridian (or N–S grid line) on the map.
3 Now rotate both map and compass until the red end of the needle points to the declination (352 degrees). The map is now set, and the terrain and map will match up.

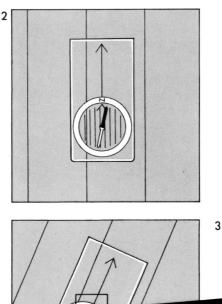

2

By pointing the compass needle at declination rather than at N, you can correct for declination without having to worry about whether you should add or subtract the necessary number of degrees. Many backpackers stick a small piece of coloured tape on the bottom of the compass capsule to show exactly where magnetic North is.

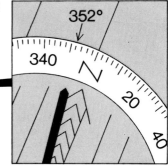

3

352°
340 N 20
40

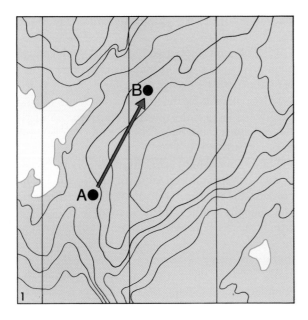

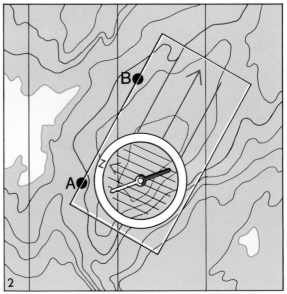

Taking a bearing from map to compass
1 Hold the map flat. Calculate the bearing with your eye; this saves you getting the final bearing 180 degrees wrong…In this example, the bearing

from **A** to **B** is about 45 degrees.

2 Place the compass along the imaginary line between **A** and **B**, with the direction-of-travel arrow pointing in that direction.

Allowing for magnetic variations
The figure shows us a simple way in which we can avoid the hassle often caused by having to remember whether we add or subtract for magnetic variations when working out compass bearings. For those who wish to know, and it is good to know these things anyway, I have included these little phrases which will help you remember when to add or subtract.
a) "Add for Mag., get rid for Grid"
b) "Grid unto Magnetic-add: GUMA"; "Magnetic unto Grid-subtract: MUGS"
c) The landscape is bigger than the map, therefore the bearing for the landscape (magnetic) should be bigger than that for the map (grid).

SIMPLE NAVIGATION
The finest compass available, as far as backpacking is concerned, is the Silva protractor compass. This type of instrument is a compass, protractor, bearing sight, straight edge, and ruler, all in one. Some Silva

Always check your bearing and position when you come to an easily recognizable feature in the terrain, for example, a bridge over a stream.

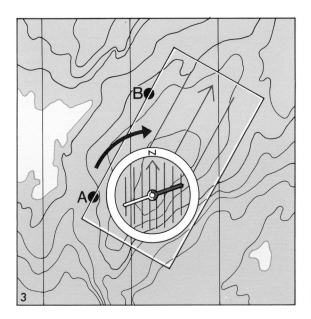

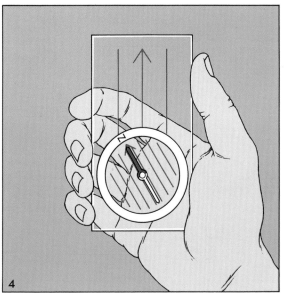

3 Turn the compass housing until the orienting lines are parallel to the map's meridians. Read off the bearing at the index mark. You now have a grid bearing. If you are in an area where the magnetic declination is more than about 3 degrees, then you need to account for it. To get a magnetic bearing, you "add for mag". That is, if the grid bearing is 46 degrees, and the magnetic declination for that map is 8 degrees, the magnetic bearing is 54 degrees. Turn the compass housing until you have this at the index mark.

4 To follow the bearing, hold the compass flat in your hand in front of you. Turn round until the red end of the needle points to N on the compass housing and is parallel to the orienting lines. The direction to walk in is now shown by the direction-of-travel line.

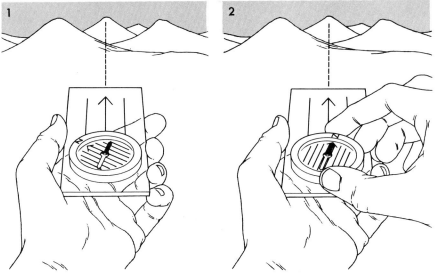

1

2

Identifying a feature
In the distance you see a hill
that you want to reach but
you cannot find it on the
map as it is one of many.
You know your exact
position on the map.
1   Point the compass's
direction-of-travel arrow
at the hill.
2   Rotate the compass
housing until the red end of
the needle points to the N
on the housing. Again,
adjust for declination, if
necessary.

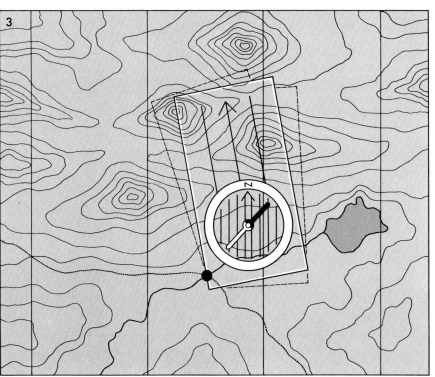

3

3   Place the long edge of
the compass on the map so
that it just touches your
position. Rotate the entire
compass until N on the
housing points to the top of
the map. For complete
accuracy, the orienting
lines on the base plate
should be parallel to the
map's meridians. Your hill
will now lie on the edge of
the compass or on a line
extending from it.

models have roamers for fixing six-figure references, and others have magnifying lenses and even
signalling mirrors. Roamers are markings on the
sides of the compass, which are used to calculate
accurate grid references.

Taking a bearing from map to compass
This is probably the most commonly used compass

exercise. If you are walking in bad visibility, fog,
low cloud, or densely falling snow, take the bearing
from the map, put it onto the compass and then
follow the compass. In the first part, that is
measuring the bearing on the map, the compass is
being used as a protractor.

When working with a compass, be extremely
careful that there are no metal objects near you

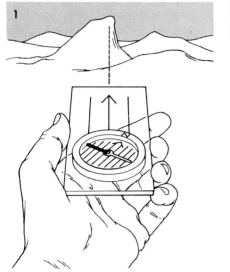

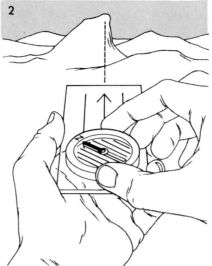

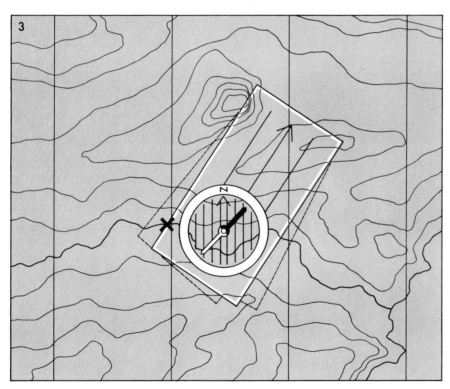

Taking a bearing from compass to map

You find yourself on a long feature, say a river or a mountain ridge, and you want to find out exactly where you are on the feature.

1 Find a feature at nearly right-angles to you that you can identify on the map. Point the direction-of-travel arrow at the feature.

2 Turn the dial until the needle points to N on the compass housing, or to magnetic N when declination is taken into account.

3 Place the long edge of the compass on the map so that it touches the feature you have just sighted on. Rotate the whole compass until the orienting lines are parallel to the meridians, with N on the compass housing pointing to the top of the map. Your position on the long feature will be where the compass edge cuts across it.

If you are not on a feature that you can find on the map, you can find your position by taking sightings like the above one, on two or three features that are identifiable on the map and drawing lines on the map. Your position is where they intersect.

which will affect its magnetism. Ice axes, watches, karabiners, and medallions could all adversely affect the magnetic needle, giving you a totally false reading.

Following the bearing
Now that we have worked out our bearing from the map, all we have to do is follow the direction of the compass's direction-of-travel arrow. Not quite that simple, I'm afraid. Imagine yourself in rough, rocky terrain. It is difficult enough walking along watching where your feet are about to land, never mind glueing your eye to the compass needle. The easiest and most accurate way of following a bearing is to select intermediary points which are on the line of travel. Cairns, odd-shaped boulders, trees, are all

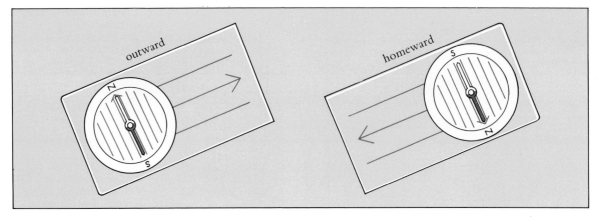

Back bearing
To return the way you have come on a bearing, or to look behind you to see if you are on course, involves the use of back bearings. Simply rotate the compass until the white end of the needle points to N or to magnetic N if you got your original bearing from the map. The direction-of-travel arrow now points in the homeward direction.

good points to fix your sights on. Find a point on the line of your direction-of-travel by looking along the line of your compass bearing. You can then put the compass away while you walk to that point. Once you have reached it, you do the same thing all over again, find another point on the direction-of-travel, and walk to it, remembering to keep it in sight. It may sound improbable, but I do know of walkers who have taken their bearing on a sheep or deer. Needless to say, the animal moves, and completely negates the direction-of-travel. Pick a point that you can easily identify, and which will not move or become suddenly obliterated by mist or fog.

Taking a bearing from compass to map
This technique, often known as resection, is used to identify features and to establish your position on the map.

Estimating time and paces
Estimating time can be thought of in two degrees of accuracy, general and detailed. Most backpackers work out a route plan before they leave home, and they generally calculate how long each stage of their trip will take. Usually, this is not particularly accurate but will give them an idea of whether the trip they have planned will be viable in the time they have allocated to it. Detailed time estimation is a different matter altogether, is usually used in foul-weather navigation, and is normally accurate to within a couple of minutes over a half-hour section.

Accurate time estimation is important in bad weather as it gives you essential information in finding your position. It tells you how far you have gone in the direction you have been travelling. When you combine accurate time estimation with accurate compass work, you can navigate in most conditions and situations.

The classic time estimation is, of course, Naismith's Rule: 3 mph plus a half-an-hour for every 1,000 feet climbed, or, in metric terms, 5 km/h plus a half-hour for every 300 metres climbed. As a general rule, this is well and good, but it is not strictly accurate. Weather, terrain, and physical fitness of the party or individual, will all have effects on the time taken and should be taken into account. Each individual backpacker should time himself as often as possible over measured sections of terrain, and, through experience, learn at what speed he or she walks. You must practice as often as possible, otherwise you are as well not to bother.

The same goes for estimating paces. The number of times you find yourself in the situation of needing such precise navigation is rare, but in very difficult conditions of poor visibility, good experience in estimating paces, combined with an accurate estimate of time, can make navigation very accurate indeed.

An average figure for an average-size man over flat ground is about 120 paces for 100 yards (90 metres). Again, the problem is to take into account the roughness of the ground, whether there is a slope or not, and how much you are carrying on your back, and again, it takes practice.

As I have said, we do not use pace estimation all that often, but when we do have to use it, it is normally in serious and potentially dangerous

Navigate by the stars

Follow the line of the pointers of the Plough (the Great Bear) and you will come to the Polar Star, which to all intents and purposes can be regarded as due North. Cassopeia is the same distance away on the other side of the Pole Star, shaped like a flattish W or M. If you cannot recognize the Plough, then forget it and go home…

(Right) An ordinary watch is useful when you need to check how long you have been hiking, but it can also be used as an emergency compass. You can find North on a sunny day by holding the watch flat in your hand, pointing the hour hand at the sun, and, ignoring the minute hand, bisecting the angle between 12 o' clock and the hour hand. The bisecting line points South. Needless to say this method does not work on a digital watch, is not accurate, and is included because if we don't include it, someone is sure to ask why…

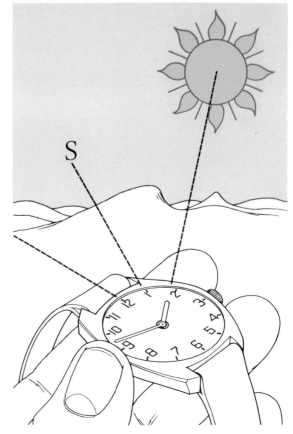

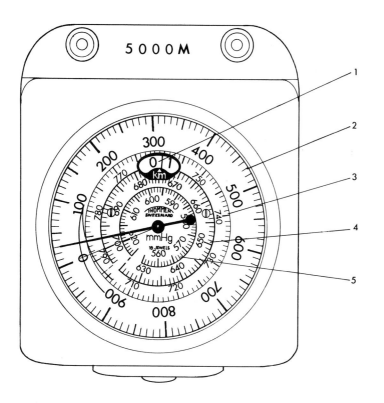

5000M

The altimeter is an extra navigational instrument that is well worth having with you in the wilderness. As it must be properly calibrated, always adjust the scale when you know exactly where you are above sea level.
(1) Scale marked in kilometres above sea level. *(2)* Scale marked in hundreds of metres. *(3)* Barometric scale marked 705-790 mm mercury. *(4)* Barometric scale marked 625-705 mm. *(5)* Barometric scale marked 555-625 mm.

An example of a practical application of the altimeter. You find yourself at a cabin whose altitude is 2,887 ft (880 m) above sea level according to the map. *(1)* Adjust the height scale to this altitude and read off the air pressure. *(2)* When you subsequently go up to a mountaintop whose altitude is 5,807 ft (1,770 m), the air pressure decreases and the altimeter indicates the new height, assuming that other conditions have not changed.

When camping out at night, you should note the air pressure as soon as you reach the campsite. If the pressure changes during the night, it shows how the weather will be: worse if the pressure drops, and better if it rises.

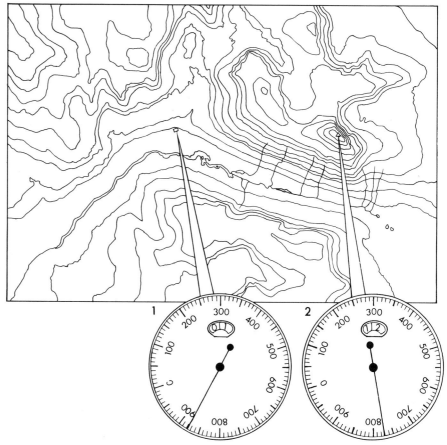

situations, so like time estimation, it has to be accurate. Orienteers have developed an astonishing accuracy with both time and pace estimation. It just shows what can be done with practice.

Altimeters

A very practical aid to navigation, especially when backpacking in mountain country, is the altimeter. This instrument works off atmospheric pressure, and it can tell you what height you are at above sea level. Its primary use is when following a well-defined feature, like a ridge or glacier. By checking the altimeter you can tell exactly at what height you are on that feature.

An altimeter must be carefully calibrated to the current atmospheric pressure, which varies quite considerably. The simplest method is to adjust the scale when you know exactly where you are and can read your height above sea level from the map.

The altimeter can also be used to keep a check on the weather situation, which depends on the air masses of high and low pressure that continually move across mountainous areas. If you notice that the indicator on the altimeter moves upwards during the night, this means a drop in atmospheric pressure and a risk of worsening weather. If the needle falls after a period of bad weather, this indicates a rise in pressure and the weather will probably improve.

Wilderness backpacking

On many of your backpacking trips it is to be hoped that the sun will smile at you, and your compass, at least, can stay happily in the top pocket of your rucksack. On good days, only a modicum of map reading is necessary to allow you to follow your progress and orientate yourself from time to time. But, when the wind picks up and visibility recedes, when the snow begins to flurry around your face in frightening squalls and your fingers grow cold and fumbling, then you draw on that old master of life, experience. The backpacker who has practised the various skills of navigation will cope. The backpacker who has decided to wait until conditions force him into action will find even the most simple acts difficult and awkward, he will forget whether to add or to subtract for magnetic variations, he may even find it difficult to hold his map properly. There are lots of things to catch the unwary unprepared, and the consequences can be tragic. Practice on the good days, and be prepared for the bad. There is a beautiful sense of achievement in navigating your

way out of trouble in bad weather; and there is immense satisfaction in knowing that you can indeed enter that hostile world of snow and wind, and know that you are competent enough to meet it on its own terms.

The time will come when even the most unadventurous backpacker will find himself confronted with other than flat, easy trail walking. There is a magnetism from the high tops which beckons most lovers of the outdoors, whether self-confessed hillmen or not, an intangible urge to climb up high, an urge that even the great George Mallory, the British mountaineer who was the leader of many attempts on Mount Everest in the 1920s, could not put into sensible words. His excuse for climbing Everest, "Because it's there", suits us well enough, although often in the course of simply walking from point *a* to point *b*, we will come across obstacles which will test our skills and strength. The basic elements of walking and camping are learned in the safe confines of well-manicured tracks and trails, where, indeed, a great many backpackers and hikers are content to stay. And why not? Backpacking to most is a therapy, not a test, and the dangers and challenges of high adventure are reserved for sky diving, hang gliding, rock climbing and white-water canoeing. Others, though, find the call of the unknown just too loud to ignore and are driven eternally upwards, if even merely for the mundane excuse of getting a good view. Others find even the hills of home too banal, and they seek far horizons, far beyond the reaches of civilisation, where indeed the elements hold the trump cards in any adventure game, and self help is the only extricating factor should things go wrong.

The middle ground between the world of the trail pounder and that of the wilderness adventurer is the subject of the next few pages. I know from hard-earned experience that rough country is not to everyone's taste, and to submit someone with natural fears and horrors to such places as tight narrow ridges, deep rivers, mountain tops, or snow-covered slopes could well knock away the foundation block of any wilderness love they may have. I clearly remember tumbling down a snow-filled cirque in the nightmare-silent arms of an avalanche. I thought I was going to die. When I realized that I was not dead, in fact not even injured, a great surge of adrenalin coursed through my body and I was ecstatic with the experience. The simple fact that I had endured that experience left me with a feeling of pathetic pride. Not so one of my companions. He also experienced the avalanche. He

Don't let the theory and techniques of the last few pages put you off! They are just a means to an end—to get you out in the wilds, in places like that shown here, and enjoying the experience, in the knowledge that you know where you are and how to get where you are going…

also survived to tell the tale, but he never set foot on a mountain again. I also recall climbing a long narrow ridge on a Scottish mountain, technically a simple climb which did not need, I thought, the security of a rope. On either side the rock plunged deeply for a thousand feet or so, and I was uplifted and greatly excited by the simple blend of exposure and the coarse granite rock which gave plenty of secure handholds and footholds. At the top of the ridge I stopped and waited for my companion, honestly expecting to hear his excited whoops of joy. When he appeared, he was clutching the rock with whitened knuckles, his face was pale, and he was sweating. As he dropped down beside me, he shook uncontrollably with fear. I spent the rest of the day nursing him back to sea level.

We are all different, thank God, and what is glorious adventure to one, may be a painful experience to another. The real test is to look carefully at a situation and say, in all honesty, that is not for me. Mountain-rescue statistics are full of people who have overreached themselves, people who have failed to appraise the situation in the light of their own experience and skill. If you do not have the experience or knowledge to know what is for you and what is not, for goodness sake don't try it unless you are with an experienced companion. Even then, you may not enjoy it, but at least the next time the situation presents itself, you will know the answer without scaring the wits from yourself.

STEEP GROUND

Movement in the mountains, as on flat trails, requires a steady rhythmic pace. If you want to move a little faster, then simply lengthen your stride, and vice versa when you want to slow down. On steep ground, the technique is the same. As the slope steepens, shorten the stride so that you can move steadily and relaxed. *Use your eyes*, look ahead and think ahead, otherwise you will tend to stop after each stride to plan the next, a painfully slow process which will slow down your forward progress to what could be a dangerous degree. Look ahead and find the best line of approach, obviously that steep cliff higher up the slope is not going to provide easy access to the summit, but what about that easy gully next to it? As you move, scan the ground a dozen yards ahead to find potential footholds, while almost simultaneously, examine the ground nearby for the next few immediate moves. Sounds complicated, but in practice, and with practice, the movements and terrain studies fall

into an automatic routine, and your pace becomes almost as quick as on a flat trail. Resist the temptation to "edge" your boots into the slope–flex your ankles so that you can place your foot flat on the ground, and then step up on it, locking out your leg at the knee after you have stepped up. With practice, and as your calf muscles become stronger, you will be able to climb steep slopes by stepping up on your toes, like an ice climber using only the front points of his crampons.

If the ground should steepen to such a degree that upwards walking becomes a great strain, then begin

The wrong way to ascend a slope. Don't lean into it. Leaning into the slope alters your centre of gravity and puts an outward and downward pressure on your boot, and your foot is more liable to slip.

tacking, or zig-zagging, your way up the slope, working out in advance where you are going to place each foot, and placing it flat on the slope for greatest traction.

When descending steep ground, similar techniques are used. Keep the stride short, keep a steady rhythm, flex your ankles, and keep your feet flat on the ground. Again, as the slope steepens, zig-zag, and think of your legs as giant coil springs, acting as shock absorbers. Don't lean too far forward, or a stumble may send you head over heels, but at the same time, don't lean back into the slope or your

feet will in all probability slip out from under you. On scree slopes, it is a great temptation to dig the heels in and run down in great bounding leaps. Scree running is great fun, but do it only when you can see the run out at the bottom, and when the scree is comprised of small stones which will move with you. Bear in mind though, that scree running is, ecologically, poor practice, and there are many large eroded hillsides in mountain areas which bear testament to generations of scree runners virtually pushing all the scree to the bottom of the mountain.

On any slope where there are loose stones, large or small, it is good practice to ensure that no member of the party is immediately below, or for that matter, above you. A dislodged stone could well find its resting place embedded in someone's head, so, if you do happen to knock a rock or stone out of place, shout "BELOW" at the top of your voice, even if you cannot see anyone immediately below you. When ascending or descending such slopes, make sure the party moves in line abreast, or in arrowhead formation. Where the route is too narrow for that, as in the case of a gully, move one at a time, while the others stay in a "safe" area.

SCRAMBLING

This is for the experienced mountain walker, only one notch away from rock climbing. Put on a medium-heavy rucksack, and what could be an easy scramble unladen, now becomes a test piece. Examine the route carefully from below, and unless you are experienced in scrambling, my advice would be to leave well alone until you get in a bit of practice on easy ground, with and without a rucksack.

Now that I have that off my mind, let me say that scrambling has given me the high point of many trips. There is an esoteric delight in using hands as well as feet, moving steadily and progressively up a steep, but well broken, rock face or ridge. There is an even more profound satisfaction in standing at the bottom again, looking upwards, and saying to yourself (or preferably to someone else), "I climbed that." The two main mistakes that most novice scramblers make are, 1) leaning into the rock, and 2) relying far too much on handholds. You may feel more secure, but it is a false sense of security.

The basic techniques for scrambling are the same as for rock climbing. Climb with your feet and legs, and use your hands mainly for balance. This is what rock climbers call "balance climbing". Keep your body weight over your feet by standing erect. The legs do the work. The handholds are not for pulling

The right way to ascend. It is more secure to lean away from the slope, so that your boots are pushing into it.

On any slope with loose rocks, ensure that no member of the party is above or below you. If you do happen to knock rocks out of place, yell "BELOW", even if you cannot see anyone below you.

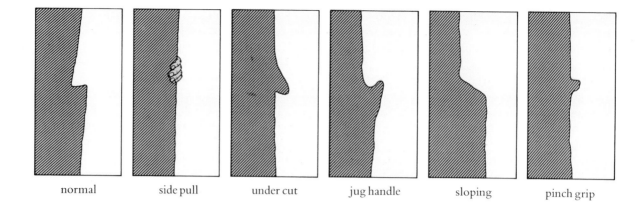

normal   side pull   under cut   jug handle   sloping   pinch grip

yourself up, but for added security should a foothold slip or come away.

Support the body at all times by having three points of contact with the rock. At all times, make sure you are in touch with the rock by two hands and a foot or two feet and a hand. In this way you will have the security of two holds should one break away or slip. Before trusting a foothold with body weight, or a handhold as an anchor, give it a kick or a bump to make sure it is firmly and totally stuck to the mountain.

Move smoothly up the rock, try not to lunge or jump for holds, and climb with the eyes. Look upwards for the next holds, and concentrate on what you are doing.

If you find yourself in a "dead-end", don't hang around like a monkey in a tree. Retreat to a safe spot and try again.

Always keep three points of contact with the rock.

Keep your body weight over your feet.

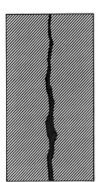

crack

Scrambling handholds

Handholds are not always immediately apparent from below, nor will they always be large, easily gripped holds which you can hang from. Some holds will require sideways pressure, some may only provide grip between thumb and fingers. Cracks in the rock may allow you to insert your fist, which, when turned sideways, may jam, offering a good firm plant. Learn to recognize different rock types, as this will affect the type of hold that you are likely to find.

Difficult scrambling terrain. Take care not to kick stones loose.

ON SNOW

When the sun shines and the snow sparkles and our spirits are soaring with the winter eagles, then winter backpacking becomes a dream. If the snow is crisp and hard, walking on it is no more difficult than walking on firm ground in summertime, so it is a good idea to start your day as early as possible, even in the dark, so that you can pack some miles in while the snow is frozen.

The main difference between summer and winter walking is that the winter variety tends to be slower, sometimes a lot slower, and you must always be on the lookout for that frustrating blend of soft and deep snow, the type that makes you wade rather than walk. Be prepared to alter your timetable too. A walk out in good hard snow conditions can change with a few hours of storm to a trudge back home again in soft unconsolidated fluff that slows you down considerably. The same goes for thaws. Sudden thaws mean swollen rivers, avalanche potential, and in some cases, crevasse danger, or, in the event of a long ski trip, a long walk carrying the skis. These possibilities should all be taken into account at the *planning* stage of your trip. Nothing is certain in winter.

Deep wet snow drops the pace to a slow wade, while firm well-consolidated snow allows fast walking on the surface. The experienced snow walker will search out the good snow surface if this is at all possible, to try and make life as easy as possible. One side of a ridge may be soft and slushy, while the other side, *the side out of the sun*, may still be hard and firm. Wooded slopes may offer firmer walking than open slopes, but, in certain circumstances, it may be the opposite way round. But after a while you will learn to recognize the snow conditions, and which type of snow is best to walk on and when. Even the colour of the snow will give you hints as to how firm it is. This is all part of snow appreciation, an art which can only be learned through experience. Snow appreciation will also allow you to recognise potential avalanche slopes.

Snow theory

Snow reaches the earth in millions of tiny, beautifully shaped crystals, which as snowfall follows snowfall, eventually accumulate on the ground as layers.

As soon as the snowflakes land, they begin a process of change known as "metamorphism". The crystals break down, the complex forms are rounded off and the beautiful feathery crystals become a mass of globules. This is a continuous process which begins at the time the snow lands on the ground and carries on until it eventually melts. Metamorphism is caused by a transfer of vapour from the points of the crystals to the more central parts. The snow crystal itself is reduced in size, but becomes much more dense. Add to this the weight of newly fallen snow on top, and the effects of a strong wind (which can even penetrate thick snow), and you will understand how a foot of snow can be reduced by a quarter or so after only a few days, without actually melting. This is known as destructive metamorphism, a somewhat confusing phrase as the snow is actually consolidating.

This settling of the snow allows the crystals to

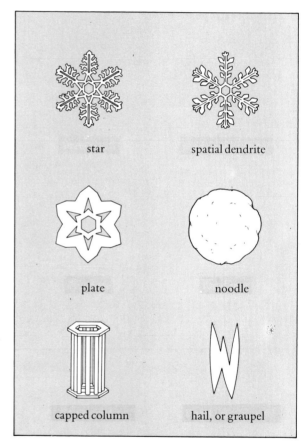

star

spatial dendrite

plate

noodle

capped column

hail, or graupel

There can be several types of snow in one fall, depending on the air temperature and the crystal type. Light-density snow in cold, dry conditions; the highest densities produce graupel, which is more or less soft hail, or needle crystals, which fall at around freezing point.

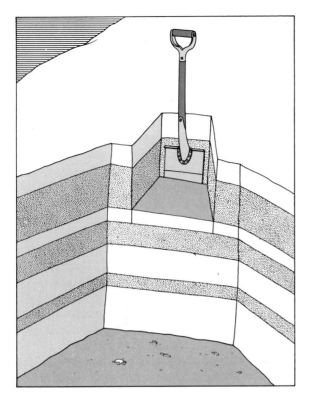

Avalanche warning test
Dig a deep pit at right angles to the wind and examine the snow layers. Check for cup crystals and depth hoar. Press your fingers into each layer to check if it is brittle or whether the layer above will slide off. If you insert the spade at the slope end of the pit and a block slides loose easily, then there is also danger of avalanche.

leads to a general toughening of the upper layers of the snow cover, at the expense of the lower layers. In very cold temperatures, depth hoar is formed in the lower layers of the cover. This depth hoar dividing the snowfall layers is potentially dangerous, as it forms an extremely fragile base for the layers above it. This danger is heightened by the fact that this type of metamorphism can take place at any depth in the layers of snow, and is likely to remain undetected unless the depth of the snow layer is examined in a sunken pit (or unless the slope avalanches). The surface layers may appear to be perfectly stable, and yet give no indication of the dangers lurking below.

Because of this poor adhesion between the layers of snow, constructive metamorphism and the resulting cup crystals can have a direct bearing on later avalanche potential. Such conditions, while possible at any time, are most common in early winter when the snow cover is shallow and still unconsolidated, and late in the season when the consolidated snow is beginning to melt.

For us winter backpackers, instability in snow is of prime importance, for snow is our medium for travelling on, and occasionally, for living in. Unstable snow which will not bear our weight, soft snow which makes walking tiresome, or packed ice which is potentially slippy are all inevitable at some time. Unstable snow which is likely to avalanche is less probably, but always inherently, dangerous. Snow, therefore, is both a friend and an enemy, and which one it is at any time depends on the climate and the snow state, and our ability in recognizing it.

Snow types
Fresh snow is of little help to us, as it gives little support, especially if it is powder snow. Beautiful for the skier, though. Old and wet snow has a bluish tinge, is unpleasant to walk on, and is avalanche prone. Old powder snow has a greyish tinge and sometimes has a crust formed by strong winds. Neve, or skare, is old hard snow, which has been melted and refrozen, or frozen and melted, time and time again. This is fine for walking on and will adhere to fairly steep slopes with little chance of avalanching.

Avalanche protection
Obviously, the best way to avoid an avalanche is to avoid snow-covered mountains, but once you commit yourself to winter backpacking, then that option is no longer open to you, so you must learn as much about avalanche protection as possible.

bond together and form a better cohesion between the layers of snow, but the bonding of crystals inside any *one* layer (that is the layer of crystals which have fallen at the same time), is stronger than the bonding between distinct layers of snow. This difference is the major cause of snow's inherent instability.

Next follows a process called constructive metamorphism. This is caused when water vapour is transferred from one part of the snow layer to another by a process known as vertical diffusion. This vapour migration causes a reduction in both the texture and the cohesion of the lower layers so that the whole snow cover is weakened from within. The vapour continues its upward travel, until it is redeposited as ice on a higher level of crystals, and builds them up in size until they become large cup-shaped crystals (cup crystals) with very poor adhesion qualities. These cup crystals are a common cause of avalanches.

In warmer climes, constructive metamorphism

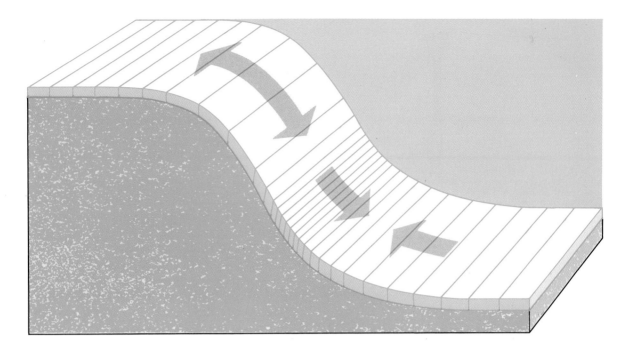

Avalanche slopes

Snow has elastic and viscous qualities. The warmer the snow, the higher the viscosity. The colder it is, the more brittle the snow mass may become. On flat ground, snow settles substantially under the stresses of further falls of snow, winds, destructive metamorphism, and gravity.

On a slope, gravity is always pulling the snow mass downhill. This settling and gravity action causes an imperceptible "creep" downhill, producing forces and stresses with the snow mass. On the convex part of a slope, the mass becomes greatly stretched, while on the

concave part, it becomes compressed. It is on the concave part that the avalanche begins. The top layer tries to pull away, thus causing a trigger point for a loose-snow avalanche or a fracture line, if it is a slab avalanche. The conclusion is that, the warmer the snow,

the more elastic it is and the greater is its ability to conform and adjust to these stresses. When the snow is cold, it is slower to adjust to these stresses. The risk for avalanche is at its greatest after a heavy snowfall, a storm, or a big change in temperature.

Find out as much as you can about the snow history of the area and familiarize yourself with different snow conditions. Avoid dangerous slopes and obvious avalanche paths like the plague, and if you really must cross a dangerous area, only expose one member of the party to it at a time. If one man is buried, then his chances of rescue are reasonably good, if his companions are not caught by the avalanche, too.

The ice axe

As far as winter backpackers are concerned, the ice axe has two major functions: as a safety tool for braking in the event of a slip on a snow slope, and as an implement for cutting steps into hard snow or icy slopes. The walker's axe tends to be rather longer than the climber's. Climbers use their axes to cut holes in confined spaces like gullies, so a shorter axe is more useful to them, while the walker's axe is more like a walking stick. The correct length for a

walker's axe is one which will just clear the ground when held straight down by your side.

Cutting steps

When the snow becomes hard, and it becomes impossible to kick steps into the slope with your boot toe, then crampons should be worn, or you must cut steps into the snow with your axe. Move diagonally across the slope and take great care as to the spacing and sizing of your steps; remember that you may have to descend them again, or your companions may use them after you. Use one hand to cut the step and let the balance and weight of the axe do the work. Hard aggressive thrusts are not necessary unless the snow is very hard indeed. Two or three blows should be enough to cut a slice from the slope large enough to take the edge of your boot. Test the step before you trust your weight to it, and keep two points of contact with the slope at any time, a foot and the ice axe.

RIVER CROSSINGS

Next to hypothermia, stream and river crossings kill more backpackers and walkers than any other cause. And yet, surprisingly, few backpackers know as much about river crossings as they do about hypothermia.

Take a look at a map of your favourite area. Chances are that your eye will immediately focus on some black dotted line, a footpath or trail, to many walkers a sign of security and safety, a way out of trouble in the event of bad weather. But what about those blue lines which cross the path from time to time? Never changing on the map, but the streams and rivers which those blue lines represent most certainly do, often with fatal results.

River and stream crossings can be the most dangerous part of a backpacking trip, and yet many backpackers are unaware there could be a problem. One of the first points to remember is that streams and rivers can change in speed, power, and size,

often in a matter of hours–even, in some parts of the world, in minutes. The pretty bubbling brook you have just stepped across could well become a raging torrent tomorrow. This is especially true in spring and early summer when the run-off from snow-melt swells the mountain streams. Similarly, a short, heavy fall of rain can dramatically enlarge the size and strength of a stream, covering up stepping stones or fords, and even sweeping man-made bridges into oblivion. Regard river crossings as an emergency procedure, and accord them that respect. Don't risk a stream crossing if there is a bridge or ford nearby. A walk upstream, for an hour or so in search of a safer crossing, is far preferable to the risk of drowning. The ability to cross a river safely is only acquired through experience, educated observation, and the recognition of different types of water course, the latter being as important as snow craft is to the ice climber or ski mountaineer. In fact, all outdoor folk have

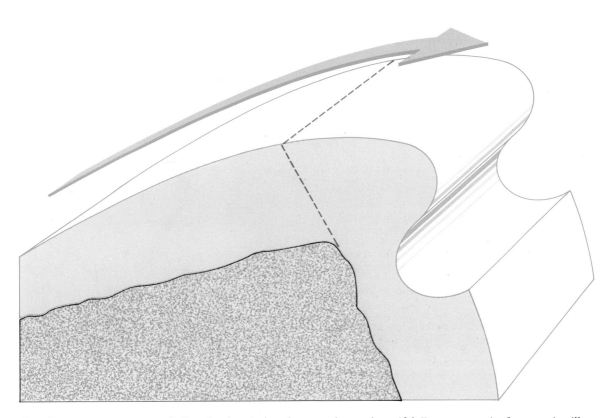

Cornices
Cornices are those often-beautiful waves of overhanging snow that are built up by the wind on the lee side of a ridge or on the top of an escarpment. They can be as dangerous as they are beautiful. Do not walk up cornices and stay well away from corniced escarpments. If the cornice fractures, it will break away at a point well behind the crest and can take you with it.

On ice and snow
(Above left) Carry your ice axe between your rucksack and your back. A walker's axe will just clear the ground if held at your side. Use a shorter axe if you are going to be climbing.

(Above right) This is the correct way to hold the ice axe when walking across or up gentle slopes. Should you slip, you simply dig in the spike.

(Right) On steep slopes, the axe shaft can be driven into the snow and used as an anchor or the head can be used as a lever to pull you up the slope.

(Opposite, left) When walking across very steep slopes, the axe should be held so that the pick can be driven into the snow quickly.

(Opposite, below left) If you fall on a steep slope, roll face into the snow across the axe and apply the pick to the snow with gradual pressure—sudden pressure will cause the axe to be snatched from your grasp. Get your head uphill and dig your boots into the snow.

(Below right) Crampons are spiked soles held to the soles of your boots by straps. They are available with ten or twelve points. On twelve-point crampons, the front pair of points sticks out like lobster claws and is used for "front pointing" up slopes.

To put a crampon on, lay it on a flat surface and open out all the straps. Check that when the straps are fastened, the buckles will be on the outside of the boot, otherwise they could cause you to trip. Place your boot in the crampon and pull the heel wire to the top of the heel-piece in your boot. The strap loops should fit snugly beside the welt of the boot. Fasten the heel strap, and then the crossover straps, pushing the last bit under the bottom of the boot lacing. This will stop the strap coming off the toe. Shake the boot around and stamp with it to ensure that the crampon is securely fastened.

Crampons should be used on icy ground, when ordinary Vibram soles become ice skates. When negotiating icy slopes, traverse rather than climb straight up. Tack, or zigzag, your way up the hill with the ice axe always at the ready. In soft snow, crampons may ball up, in which case give them a firm rap with your axe. If it happens continually, take them off, as they can become slippery.

(Inset) Practice walking in crampons, up, down, and across slopes. Flex your ankles to accommodate the angle of the surface, and walk with a slight stamping action, so that all the crampon points bite simultaneously.

more in common than we think. This is borne out when river and steam crossings come under our observation: we walkers and backpackers should look at rivers through the eyes of a canoeist... The decision to cross a river at a particular point, or not to cross, depends entirely on the individual's assessment of the depth, speed and power of the water. All rivers vary in type and a fast flowing river with a smooth shingle bottom may be easier to cross than a languid one with a bottom of greasy slippery rocks.

Generally, the wider the river is, the more the water is likely to be shallow and slow moving. Check for shingle or sand bars, as this often gives a clue as to where the mature river begins to drop down a gradient. Where the mature river runs in a meander, the bends are likely to be deeper. Try and choose a high vantage point, and examine the course of the river, looking out for eddies and turbulence.

When choosing a ford, stop and assess the situation. Check such things as the colour of the water, whether the material in the bed of the river is

Generally speaking, there are three types of river. The high-level, fast-flowing, immature stream **(above)** usually has a bed of rocks and boulders, some submerged, some visible. All of these create eddies, currents, turbulence, and white water. In spring and early summer, the stream may be fed by snow-melt and increase dramatically in volume. Crossing these streams is normally not difficult, but you ought to use a safety line if you are crossing above rough and possibly deep waters **(opposite, above)**. The second type of river is more mature and will not flow so fast. Such rivers are found lower down the valleys, where the slope is less. Often, they have a bed of shingle or small rocks which looks reasonably safe to walk on,

but you should take into account the speed of the flow. Further down the valley we find the third type, when the river has become stately and serene **(opposite, bottom)**. It can very well be deep, even if it is slow-moving.

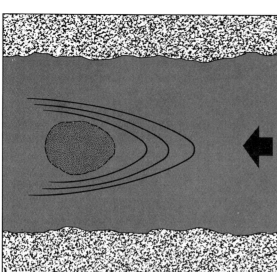

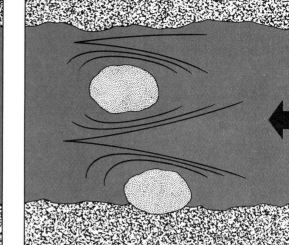

Reading a river
Submerged rocks cause the water to ripple in a V-shape **(Left)**, the apex of the V pointing upstream. If the boulders are deeply submerged then a series of largish standing waves will indicate this.

(Right) Two submerged or partially submerged rocks will produce a V-shape pointing downstream, showing where the main flow of water is. If the V is fairly narrow, it may be that you can use to advantage the horizontal eddies behind the rocks, where the water is more placid. By crossing here, you can wade in the protection of the rocks, force the narrow main current, and come into the protection of the next rock. Great caution is necessary, though.

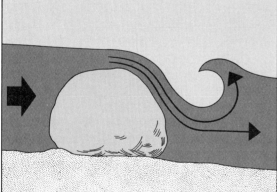

When there is a large rock just below the surface, "stoppers" are formed by the water running over it, forming what is practically a waterfall on the downstream side. The current runs over the rock, is forced down deep and almost comes back on itself in the form of a vertical eddy. This stopper is extremely dangerous, and if you are caught in one, the chances are that you will be trapped and drown. Theoretically, escape from a stopper can be achieved if you drop to the river bottom and let the current sweep you downstream. Great lungfuls of air are a distinct advantage…

being shifted by the force of the current, the width of the river, and the speed and volume of the water. If you can hear a distinct rumbling over and above the crashing of the water, it is likely to be boulders and rocks being trundled along the bottom by the power of the watercourse. Avoid a crossing here, and likewise if branches or logs are being visibly swept along. Don't try a ford where there are large rocks, slippery smooth slabs, sand, or mud. High overhanging banks are a sure sign that the water is running deep and fast.

Stream beds of shingle or gravel, or even of small stable rocks, offer the safest forms of fording, but check that the outflow of such an area is reasonably free of obstructions too. Walkers have been drowned by stumbling in safe fords, and then being swept downstream and trapped against large rocks. Most mountain streams are crossed by boulder hopping, but don't bite off more than you can chew. Assess the situation continually, and remember that big leaps are impossible when wearing a heavy pack. Check in cold weather that the rocks are not glazed in verglas, water ice, and don't try to boulder hop if you suspect the rocks may be slippy with slime.

Fast-flowing deep rivers can sometimes be

River crossings
(Top) Several hikers, crossing together, can support each other by forming a circle of three. The heaviest person faces upstream, linking arms with the other two, who link arms with each other and face inward, so that all three are linked by the arms, with heads together and feet apart. The trio forms, in other words, a triangle of support. Only one should move at a time, with the others supporting. In really heavy water, however, it may be best for all three to move together.

(Below) The group can also cross by using a long branch or a walking staff as shown—side by side, with arms interlocked and each hiker holding onto the branch or staff. They move together, giving mutual support.

crossed by diverting your route uphill and finding a point where the stream is narrower. Route diversions of an hour or two are not unreasonable, especially under conditions of thaw or spate. And don't forget the obvious: check the map to see if there is a bridge nearby.

Once you have selected a likely crossing point, you must choose the method of crossing. If you are alone, or if the ford looks reasonably safe with secure footing, stop and take off your socks; there is little point in getting them soaked. Put your boots back on bare feet for the wade. The boots will afford you some protection from injury and the cold, and you will get a better grip on the river-bed surface. I once had the unpleasant experience of wading a wide, fairly slow-moving stream, in my bare feet, and stumbling halfway across because my feet had gone numb and I could not feel the rocks on the bottom. On another occasion, in a fit of mind-storming smartassed-ness, I took my boots off and, rather than carry them, I heaved them across the stream to the far bank, only to see them fall short and float off downstream. If you are wearing a pack, undo the hip harness so that the pack can be jettisoned quickly should you fall. If you are carried off on the current, the weight and buoyancy of the pack will force your face down on the water. Not an inviting prospect. Don't hesitate to shed it if you must. Knickers are better than baggy long trousers, which tend to offer a greater resistance to the water flow. Take off long trousers, but keep on long johns or thermal underwear if the water is very cold for some extra protection.

Start wading into the stream, preferably sideways into the current. Don't be tempted into facing downstream as the force of the current could well buckle your legs at the knee. Move one foot at a time, take it easy, and shuffle your way across rather than take large steps. Only move a foot when the other is firmly placed, don't cross the legs over, but keep them apart, stable and braced. It may be a good idea to find a long stick to be used as a third leg. Use the stick as a support on the upstream side, keep a two-point contact when moving, just as you would use an ice axe when kicking steps up a snow slope.

If the river is placid and deep, it may be possible to swim across. Use your pack as a buoyancy aid by wrapping all your gear in plastic bags, and tying the ends tight shut. Invert saucepans, and tie the top of the bag down as tightly as possible. Float your rucksack buoyancy aid in front of you and swim across by kicking your legs, across and slightly downstream in a form of "ferry glide".

In cool weather, someone may get himself dangerously chilled. In that event you may have to strip him, dry him, and get him into a warmed sleeping bag, following the drill for hypothermia. If the chill is not that serious, cram as much starch and sugar into him as possible, and start walking fast and hard in order to produce as much body heat as possible. Wet clothes dry out surprisingly quickly when you move fast.

If you unfortunately happen to get swept away, keep calm, get rid of your rucksack by slipping it off your shoulders, and try to get into a position where you can float feet first downstream. Use your feet to fend off rocks, and try to swim across the current rather than against it, in the hope that you may float into a quiet backwater or eddy out of the main current. Beware of log jams or sunken trees, as you could very easily become trapped under the water, where the force of the current will hold you under.

River crossings are an unavoidable part of any backpacking itinerary, and the current state of the art should be studied with the same thoroughness as a winter climber studies avalanches. Being swept down in an avalanche and being swept away by a river have much in common, except that in an avalanche there is always the lucky chance that someone will be able to dig you out alive. The odds are not so great after you have been battered and bashed against a few rocks in a fast-flowing river.

LIGHTNING

Very few backpackers are killed by lightning strikes, and according to the law of averages, very few backpackers are likely to be struck by lightning. But, the reason I have included the subject in this book is because the law of averages is about the only defence most backpackers have against it. It is a subject which, because of its unlikelihood, is largely ignored, and that is no protection at all.

Lightning, like avalanches, should be regarded as a source of potential objective danger.

Lightning is caused by electrical energy in the atmosphere, and electricity flows along the line of least resistance. Any break in the conductor, that is the material through which it flows, will cause the current to jump across the gap, just like the spark plug in a car. During thunderstorms, clouds become charged with electricity, which then jumps the shortest possible distance to earth with a flash of light, invariably striking the most prominent feature on the terrain.

There are three varieties of lightning. The first tends to occur within the cloud, from cloud to cloud, or from charged air down to a cloud. This phenomenon is interesting, but offers no real threat to us as backpackers. The second, and most frequent variety, is called downstroke lightning, because it travels from the cloud down to the earth, usually striking the most prominent object on the terrain. This downstroke may, rarely, hit someone directly, but more often than not it causes a voltage-robbing "breakdown" in the air surrounding the body, so that the individual only has to endure a few thousand volts of what is known as arc-voltage for an extreme fraction of a second. While that can be enough to cause death, it rarely is, and the victim normally fully recovers fairly quickly. Upward-stroke lightning is a different ball game. Here, the lightning begins on the ground and shoots upwards to the clouds. This kind of strike tends to be limited to the tops of mountains, so backpackers and climbers are at risk. A person struck by upward-stroke lightning may draw as many as 300 amperes for several hundredths of a second, at a temperature of up to 50,000 degrees F. This combination of electrical shock, plus external heating, almost always results in cardiac arrest. Typically, burns are usually found on the body, and metal zippers or buttons may become welded together. So what do we do if caught in an electrical storm? Unless you are very unlucky, you should be able to notice the storm approaching. You will probably hear thunder, and you may even feel the electricity in the air; your hair may stand on end, your skin may prickle, and your ice axe may start humming and sparking and show a bluish glow...

Because lightning invariably strikes the prominent features on the ground, there are zones which are less likely to be hit. The ideal place to be is away from all steel objects, crouched low on your knees with your feet held together. If possible, put some insulation between you and the ground, either coiled ropes, or sleeping pads, or your rucksack (provided there are no metal attachments on it, and you have emptied out pots, stoves, tentpoles, tent pegs, etc).

The aim is to have the least contact possible with the ground. You should be well away from exposed ridges, mountain tops, prominent boulders, and cairns. Don't try and find protection in gullies, shallow caves, or under overhanging rocks, as features like these tend to act as the spark-plug gaps, and you could suffer severe burns.

COPING WITH THE HOT

In winter, it is obvious that we will wrap up warm

against the cold. The winds and frost, snow and storms rarely allow us to forget their presence. Staying warm in the cold is very necessary, but so too is staying cool in the hot. Few backpackers understand heat prostration or heat stroke, the hot weather equivalent of hypothermia: *hyperthermia*.

Hyperthermia strikes suddenly and swiftly as soon as the body's cooling system decides to shut down.

When the weather is particularly hot and humid, your body loses its fluids (in the form of sweat) faster than you can replace them. Backpackers must constantly guard against hyperthermia, especially in desert areas, on beach walks in hot weather, and on mountains when the weather is particularly hot. Consider at the trip-planning stage how available water supplies will be, and if it is at all likely that you may run short, then you will have to carry it with you. You must drink an adequate supply of the stuff: 2 quarts (about 2 l) of water are lost by your body, *per hour*, in really hot temperatures. That means a lot of water has to be quaffed to replace it.

Wear light-coloured clothing if at all possible. Remember that darker shades absorb heat while lighter ones reflect it. Cotton, despised by backpackers in winter, is welcome in summer because it is a lot lighter than wool, and it has the capability of wicking moisture away from the skin at a fast rate, keeping the skin cool, but not chilled.

Keep your arms and neck covered, legs too unless you are used to walking in shorts. Wear sunglasses, especially if there is snow about, or if you are walking on brightly coloured sand, to combat ultra-violet reflection. The eyes are extremely

sensitive things, and great care must be taken for their protection.

If your skin is at all sensitive to sun, then smear on plenty of sunscreen cream for protection. Wear a hat, or even a bandana knotted at the corners, to protect the scalp, and it is often a good idea to let a bandana or a small towel hang down the back of your neck, Foreign Legion style.

COPING WITH THE COLD

One of the major problems in backpacking in winter is keeping warm and dry. Backpacking, skiing, or even snowshoe-ing are all fairly strenuous activities, and while you may be warm, even hot, when active, you will rapidly cool down when you stop for a break. Many authorities will tell you that it is inadvisable to break sweat in winter, as the moisture will dampen your clothing, which leads eventually to chilling. This is all very well, but try telling your body that as you struggle up a mountain slope with a heavy rucksack on your back… It is far better to try and balance heat production and heat loss by the proper use of zips, opening up for ventilation when you become hot, and putting on the really warm and windproof gear at rest stops when chilling can take place within minutes.

Keeping dry is another problem. If it is snowing, you are better wearing smooth-surfaced garments like nylon, from which the flakes will slide off before they get a chance to melt. Brush off any snow which begins to accumulate on your clothing, but be careful that the snow, melting off your jacket, does not soak your trousers. Knock snow from tree branches before you pass under them, for your pack may just happen to catch them as you pass below, dumping a load of snow on top of you.

Eat plenty of carbohydrates as you walk along. Chocolate, boiled sweets and glucose sweets all help to maintain body warmth and energy.

Windchill
Beware the wind. Even comparatively small amounts of wind have chilling effects on the body because they carry away the thin layer of warm air which builds up near the body. Increasing wind speeds up to 40 mph (64 km/h) have the effect of lowering the temperature and although after this speed there is little additional effect, you will by then have had quite enough… Low temperatures themselves are little problem if you are adequately clad and can keep on the move, but if the wind rises, then the effective temperature becomes much lower than the true air temperature.

When the temperature is below freezing, carry your water bottle upside down in your pack, so that any ice that forms cannot plug the neck. If the weather is extremely cold, wrap the bottle in a sweater. When backpacking in the cold you should try to drink warm drinks such as fruit "soup" or tea. Cold drinks require body heat to warm them, and coffee is a diuretic and reduces your body water.

Wind and temperature

Wind speed mph	Local temperature (°F)			
0	32	23	14	5
5	29	20	10	1
10	18	7	-4	-15
15	13	-1	-13	-25
20	7	-6	-19	-32
30	1	-13	-27	-41

Wind speed m/s	Local temperature (°C)			
0	0	-5	-10	-15
2.25	-2	-7	-12	-17
4.5	-8	-14	-20	-26
6.75	-11	-18	-25	-32
9	-14	-21	-28	-36
13.5	-17	-25	-33	-41

The big danger to winter backpackers is the wind. For example, at an actual thermometer reading of 5°F (-15°C) and with a wind speed of 10 mph (4.5 metres per second), the effective temperatures drops to -15°F (-26°C), a temperature almost low enough for exposed flesh to freeze. If you are not prepared for winter winds, you could get into serious trouble. Wear windproof clothes, use a lip salve and a barrier cream on your face, and keep your head, hands, and ears covered.

Exposure

Exposure, or more correctly, hypothermia, is often encountered in wet-cold conditions. When the body becomes chilled, it begins to reduce circulation to the skin and to the extremities in order to maintain the proper temperature in the vital organs. This middle part of the body, the inner core, must be kept at a steady temperature. In normal conditions, the inner core remains at a constant 98.4°F (36.9°C), and the preservation of this inner-core temperature is vital.

A fall in the core temperature leads to mental deterioration, loss of muscular control, eventual unconsciousness, and then death. A fair definition of hypothermia could be: Severe chilling of the body surface leading to a progressive fall in body-core temperature with the risk of death.

People die from exposure in places other than mountains. Old folk often succumb to the winter cold in under-heated homes, and immersion in cold water leads to a quick cooling-off of the inner core resulting in death. In the mountains, cold alone rarely kills, but when cold is coupled with depleted energy reserves, or simply tiredness, the body can no longer keep a stable temperature, and exposure can follow. It is essential to preserve a sufficient reserve of energy in severe conditions of high wind, cold, and wet.

Overestimation of fitness as well as underestimation of the time needed to reach a destination are common subsidiary causes of exposure. Inadequate diet is another. The human body is like a machine and constantly needs fuel to keep it going. The harder you push your body, the more fuel you need, and on a hard winter hike your energy needs could rise to 7,000 calories or more a day. Your kit should contain a high-energy snack lunch to be eaten on the trail.

It is not always easy to decide when you have a case of exposure on your hands. It is even more difficult to realize when you yourself are becoming a victim. Watch your companions, and ask them to keep a watch on you. If you suspect the early symptoms of exposure you may be able to avoid a crisis later on.

A hypothermia victim will generally prove to be awkward, both in his movements and attitude. Unreasonable behaviour and complaints of coldness and fatigue may be signs that exposure is taking place. He may start shivering, stumble, speak with a slurred voice, have sudden violent outbursts of energy, and may react aggressively to suggestions that he stops walking and takes shelter. It should be emphasized that under difficult conditions members of a party should keep close together and watch each other carefully. Stay alert.

As soon as the symptoms are established, stop. If the victim has collapsed and become unconscious, send for help, for the situation is extremely serious. Maintaining the temperature of the inner core is vital. Bearing this in mind, it is folly to cause the blood to circulate in the extremities of the body surface by rubbing, or adding surface warmth. The inner core needs the blood circulating down there. The first consideration should be to insulate the victim from the elements and use every means possible to keep his inner-core temperature stable. Then re-warm the victim. If he is wet, remove the wet clothes, dry him without rubbing, and put him into a *prewarmed* sleeping bag. Pitch a tent for shelter. A freshly unpacked sleeping bag is not much good, as the victim just will not have the body heat to warm it up, so put a fit companion inside the sleeping bag also to give added warmth. Pay particular attention to the ground insulation, and make sure there is a wind- and waterproof covering around the bag, either a tent or a survival bag. If he can take food, limit it to sweet, warm but not hot, drinks, given in small swallows. Never force alcohol into an unconscious person. The blood supply to the stomach at this stage is so limited that heavy foods will not be digested. Keep the victim warm until help arrives, even if he apparently recovers and insists on carrying on.

Frostbite

Frostbite and exposure are closely related. One of the body's first reactions to severe chill is to cut off the circulation to the extremities, in order to preserve heat at the body core. This reduces the blood supply to toes, fingers, and the other extremities, and it provides ready access for frostbite. Frostbite problems usually occur when temperatures are abnormally low, or when someone gets wet or is forced to bivouac in very bad weather.

Frostbite is an injury resulting from a freezing of the tissues, which usually occurs in the hands, feet, or face, but rarely anywhere else. It can be avoided by applying reasonable care. In addition to the maintenance of general body warmth, pay careful

Heat loss factors include lack of physical conditioning, wind, low temperatures, and wet and damp caused by rain, sweat, or snow.

Radiation. An uncovered head can lose up to 50% of its body-heat production at 40°F (4.4°C) and 75% at 5°F (–15°C).

Conduction. Touching cold objects, sitting on snow or stones.

Convection. Air movement, however imperceptible, carries away body heat. Wind-chill temperatures are dramatically lower than regular temperatures (see opposite).

Evaporation. Also known as sweating. Ventilate your clothes as much as possible during periods of high energy output.

Respiration. Heat is lost when inhaled air is raised to body temperature.

attention to the state of your hands and feet. Tight-fitting clothing or tight boot lacing which cuts circulation should be avoided. Tight rucksack shoulder straps can be another contributing factor. Painfully cold feet or hands which suddenly cease to hurt should be taken care of immediately, but it is better to keep them warm, even though it means taking off gaiters, boots, and socks. If the warning signs are ignored, a long and painful process of frostbite may occur with the possibility of tissue loss and crippled limbs.

Prevention is better than cure, so avoid tight boots and clothing which restrict circulation, and keep the extremities warm.

Should frostbite really set in, the affected part will appear white and will feel like cold stone. If the freezing continues the part will go numb, but then feel warm. This warmth is an illusion, and indicates a very serious stage of frostbite, when tissue injury is inevitable. If at all possible, the victim should be taken to medical help. If it is the feet which are frozen, then he should be treated as a stretcher case. Never expect someone with frostbitten feet to walk

Learn to read the clouds. Experience is the best teacher, but if you go hiking with a knowledgable companion, you can pick up weather lore from him or her. **(Far left)** These light clouds are beginning to thicken into a piled cumulus formation. **(Below)** The piled cumulus clouds have developed and now indicate unstable weather, as when cold and warm air masses meet. Stratus clouds form the background.

(Above) Altocumulus clouds are usually arranged in waves or lines, and normally indicate fairly stable weather. Should they become more compact, there is risk for some local showers.

unless it is absolutely necessary. Although it may be possible to walk on frozen feet, it will be impossible to walk once they have been rewarmed, when the pain is severe. Do not, under any circumstances, rub the affected part with snow. That will only cause further damage.

The frozen part must be thawed out all at once, rather than gradually, and preferably under medical supervision. Heat some water until it is tepid, about 108°F (40°C). If you do not have a thermometer, test the water by dipping your elbow in it. It should feel pleasantly warm. Keeping the water at that temperature, soak the part for twenty to thirty minutes. Don't be tempted to massage the affected part, to break any blisters which have formed, or to exercise the limb. As soon as possible, get the victim to a hospital, making sure that the injured part is well protected.

PERSONAL WEATHER FORECASTING

The weather is important to us all, even if just as a topic of conversation, but to the backpacker, whose world is the outdoors, weather quite often can be a gauge of our personal spirits. When the weather is good, we feel good, and as the barometer drops, so our spirits tend to drop too; personal feelings and barometric pressure are tied inextricably together.

As the weather is something we can do very little about, we may as well grin and bear it. On the other hand, it does not pay to ignore it altogether. We must be prepared for it, especially the bad variety, as it could dictate more than just our feelings for a few days. In backpacking, the weather is very much our master, and it can control in fairly large degrees just how far we can walk, where we can walk, where we can camp, and more important, where we cannot camp. So it makes sense to try and prophesy

in advance just what the weather gods have up their sleeve.

Weather forecasts are available from a large number of sources: television, radio, newspapers, and meteorological centres. Few of these outlets are of much use to backpackers, unless they carry a small radio, and this is one darned good excuse for carrying a radio with you...

Of infinitely more value is the development of personal weather-forecasting skills. If you have a natural apathy to words like "fronts", "depressions", "falling pressure", and "anticyclones", then I apologize, but you are going to have to get used to them. Listen as often as you can to the weather forecast on television or radio before you set out. Look out for key words which herald bad weather in the mountains: fronts, troughs, depressions, low pressure, falling pressure, increasing cloud/wind. Listen, too, for words which mean good weather in the hills; words like calm or light winds, high pressure, anticyclone, rising pressure, clear skies, fog and/or frost warnings.

Make a habit of reading the weather forecasts, note what they are, and then carefully watch the weather. Get to know what the various terms used by weather forecasters are, and how to recognise them. At the same time, try to identify clouds by reference to pictures. Having listened to the forecasts for several weeks, and having noted the weather in that time, try and make your own forecasts by observing the weather patterns. Check your results with the regular weather forecasts. The key to weather forecasting is to look at the weather regularly, read the weather maps, and compare what you see with what is happening, and what happens later, outside. "Keep a weather eye open" is an age-old saying, but it does pay dividends when the weather is so important to us.

Chap. 4

LIVING OUTDOORS

Backpacking, it has been suggested, is an activity for masochists. To pack and carry a rucksack which then weighs upwards of thirty pounds or so, and to carry it to some obscure mountain top for the pleasure of sleeping on hard uncompromising ground, only to get up in the morning, put on damp clothes, and do the whole damned thing all over again…

I am in the business of telling people that this vision they have of backpacking is totally erroneous. It is my job to convert the non-believers, to glamourize the physical side and romanticize on the mental side. But I have this sneaking belief that if you honestly and truly believe that backpacking is all grit and pain and discomfort, then you will never, and I repeat never, experience the positive and pleasurable side.

Lightweight comfort

The great challenge in backpacking does not lie so much in walking skill or camping skill, but in being able to minimize the amount of equipment you carry on your back, without sacrificing camping comfort. This sounds like an anomaly, but such are the advances in camping equipment in recent years, that a very high comfort level can be maintained without breaking your back. The novice backpacker will load his rucksack with every contrivance under the sun, fully believing that he cannot step away from the trailhead without his various bits and pieces. A good test is to tip everything out of your rucksack when you come home, and lay aside everything you did not use. Look at these items carefully, and decide, with all honesty, whether they have a rightful place in your pack in the future. You will be surprised how much "necessary" gear you throw away.

The continual paring of ounces will prove beneficial in the long run. I am fully aware that there is not all that much difference between a 20-lb (9 kg) rucksack and a 23-lb (10.5 kg) rucksack, but that is not really the point. The major point is that if you are not aware of weight, if you do not continually scourge weight from your rucksack, then your pack load will increase and increase until you will be carrying very heavy loads, even on short summer trips. The lesson is to be *aware* of weight.

So how can weight be saved? Obviously, weight accrues easily on items like tents, sleeping bags, stoves, and food. Be conscious of the weight of these items when you buy them. You do not need a three-man tent if you intend backpacking solo most of the time. You do not need a Himalayan sleeping-bag if you only backpack in the summer. You do not need a heavy pressurised petrol stove if you only intend walking some low-level footpaths during the odd weekend. Don't shop with the thoughts of that high-level, long-distance route you may do sometime in the future. Shop with the thoughts of the trips you do week in and week out; no doubt you will buy special gear for that big trip to Alaska, or Lapland, or the Himalayas.

Ounces easily turn into pounds, so be aware of the little items. Backpackers are renowned for their weight-paring habits, and it makes a good game, especially if you have some youngsters along. See who can think up the most ingenious methods of saving weight.

Saw the handle off your toothbrush. Sounds silly but will save a bit of weight. Take the concept a little bit further and carry only candle stubs to see you through the dark hours you will spend away from home, instead of full-size candles which you will probably have to carry home again. The same theory can apply to note-taking gear. Carry only a stub of a pencil rather than a heavier pen, and carry

There is a wonderful freedom in travelling light—
with a day pack and just
the basics in clothing and
equipment. In mountain
areas like this, the light
backpacker should always
keep a weather eye open
and plan the route so that
some kind of shelter is
within reasonable dis-
tance. Not so the hiker
(inset) with a heavy frame
pack, covered with a rain-
proof poncho and with a
strong walking staff; he is
well prepared for all even-
tualities.

little notelets instead of a full-blown notebook. By now you could have saved ½ lb (¼ kg). It is amazing how much of the little bits and pieces we carry on the trail with us are mere cosmetic. Some of these can be cut off, sawn off, or broken off, and still be functional. Have a look at your kit and see how you can lighten it.

Cut the legs of a pair of trousers, above the knee. Sew a strip of Velcro or a zipper at the cuts so that one pair of trousers can be used as longs, or shorts. This saves you carrying extra weight.... The same can be done with shirts, although most folk merely roll up their sleeves. Some manufacturers produce insulated jackets with zippered inserts at the top of the sleeves so that you can take the sleeves off, and use the jacket as an insulated vest when the weather warms up. Again, you save the weight of carrying two garments.

Trim the margins off your paperback book, and burn the pages as you finish reading them. Also a good source of toilet paper; again, this saves weight. If you read hardback books, take the heavy covers off and leave them at home. Many backpackers I know spend a lot of time scouring second-hand bookshops for cheap books which can be ripped up and disposed of as they walk through their backpacking trip. The quicker you read, the lighter your pack will be.

Share a razor amongst the men who want to shave, and carry only some extra blades. Better still, grow a beard. I grew a beard over twelve years ago while on a backpacking trip, and I still have it. Apart from saving on the weight of shaving kit, a beard saves time in the mornings (at home, too!). Nobody really worries too much what you look like when you are backpacking, and sartorial elegance will not improve your backpacking skill or technique. In a childish sort of way, I rather enjoy being a bit tatty (the windswept look...) on the trail. Go into your bathroom now and pick up your razor, shaving brush, soap, and, if you insist on using it, after-shave lotion. Weigh them on the kitchen scales, and I think you will be surprised at the weight of it all. After shave lotion, incidentally, tends to attract a lot of unwanted biting insects like mosquitos, blackfly, midges, etc. The same goes for women's eau-de-cologne and perfume.

Remove the cardboard core from toilet paper, towels, and the cardboard backing from books of matches, food, etc. Cardboard packaging is heavy and is mostly merely cosmetic. Cardboard boxes also take up a lot of space in your pack. Use plastic bags instead. They are far more useful, can be used over and over again, and weigh virtually nothing. Make sure that you label them though. Potato powder looks very similar to dried milk, and potato powder in your coffee is not pleasant.

As you finish toothpaste, soap, toilet paper, etc., at home, leave just enough for your next backpacking trip. If you head out for a weekend trip, it is pointless carrying a full tube of toothpaste, or a full bar of soap, which tends to be very heavy anyway. Carry only enough to last the length of your trip. Get others to do the same for you, and you will soon have a fine little collection. In fact, why bother with toothpaste, soap, and toilet paper? I tend to use salt for brushing my teeth on trips, and I rarely carry soap. I like to think that soap is ecologically unsound. Just watch someone lathering himself or herself in a mountain stream and watch the suds float away. Someone downstream could be collecting that water for cooking or drinking. That is my excuse for not using soap, and I stick to it. As I have already made clear, I am not too worried about getting a bit dirty, although it is amazing how clean you can become with honest-to-goodness cold water. Toilet paper is merely a luxury. Remember the paperback books? Or try snow, leaves, grass, or mosses.

Carry only one spare sock, so that you are always wearing two while washing or drying the third. It helps if the three of your socks are the same colour. Change your socks around, from the left foot to the right and vice versa. It is almost like putting on fresh ones. Then turn them inside out and wear them like that. You very quickly get into the habit of washing the extra sock every night, and one sock is a lot easier to dry than two...

If you have cuffs, or turn-ups, on your trousers, cut them off. Cuffs are pointless and useless. All they do is gather twigs, soil, heather, pebbles, or snow, which further increases the weight you have to carry.

Remove any fittings from your pack that you do not use. Modern packs usually come fitted with a vast array of straps, buckles, internal frames, cushioning, etc. Many of these you will not need. For example, there is little point in having ice-axe loops on a pack that you will only use during the summer months. Many packs come fitted with loops and straps for rock-climbing paraphernalia. Most backpackers will not need them, so cut them off. Softpacks are lighter in weight than frame packs, so try your pack with the frame taken out. You will probably have to spend a little bit longer packing your gear into it, so that you do not have items digging into the small of your back, but it is worth the effort for the weight that can be saved. Experiment at home before you head out on the trail.

For mixing drinks or powdered milk, use a plastic bag instead of a plastic bottle. As I have already suggested, plastic bags are the backpacker's best friend. It is well worth while carrying a few spare ones, and even a dozen plastic bags are lighter in weight than one single plastic bottle.

Eat straight from the pot. You do not need plates. Most of your meals will be one-pot meals anyway, so you may as well eat straight from the pot. Plates are only extra weight, and extra things to wash up. The same goes for eating utensils. A single spoon and a knife are all that is necessary. A fork is one of modern man's most useless inventions and is completely out of place in a backpacking kit. My sole concession to luxury in my eating and cooking kit is a tea spoon. Somehow I can never gauge the correct amount of sugar for my tea or coffee from a big camping spoon. A tea spoon makes me feel quite posh.

Load your pack a week or so before leaving home, and then weigh it every day. You will be surprised how many things you will leave at home in an effort to cut weight. Think of yourself climbing a long hill in the sun, and then consider if it is worth while carrying that heavy two-volume book, or the extra socks and sweaters. At the end of your trip, turn out your pack and look out everything you have not used. With the exception of emergency rations and your first-aid kit, throw the rest away, and don't pack it again unless you are sure you will need to use it.

Needless to say, common sense plays an important part in this weight-paring game. Never leave essentials at home, and by essentials I mean protective clothing, food, something to cook it on, fuel, and a sleeping-bag. Some sort of overnight protection is also necessary most of the time, even if that protection is just a plastic bivouac bag. Make out a check list of the essentials, and refer to it every time you pack for a trip.

Without a tent

Many backpackers save themselves a lot of weight by leaving their tent at home. In areas where there are mountain huts, lean-tos, youth hostels, caves or other natural shelters, this may be a good idea. But bear in mind that the mountain hut you are making for may be full of like-minded souls, and the solitude you have been relishing may be filled of laughter, song, or even argument, maybe into the early hours. Gregarious backpackers may enjoy

that: I can find that atmosphere in my local pub. You cannot choose your company in a hut, or a youth hostel, and hotels and guest houses tie you to set times and rules. By limiting yourself to a set distance each day, to tie in with the opening hours of your guest house or hostel or whatever, and then by rushing to get there before it becomes full, you strip yourself of the freedom and mobility that a tent offers. To make camp when you are tired, or when the view is nice, or when it begins to rain, is the most marvellous thing about backpacking: the sheer untrammelled freedom.

There is another alternative to a tent: the bivouac. By using a long plastic bag, or a tarp, it is often possible to rig up a simple, but effective shelter. These shelters do not provide the weatherproofness of a good-quality tent, but when you consider the relative costs, you will not be surprised. (Tarps are probably a tenth of the cost of even a cheap tent.)

Bivouac bag (bivvy bags) made of Gore-Tex are another alternative to the tent, and, although they are expensive, they are growing in popularity among backpackers who want to go lightweight and to sleep out. The hooped bivvy bag is really a tiny tent, functional but with the minimum of comfort.

Nights in the open

I know of hardened hill walkers and mountain climbers who shudder at the thought of spending a night outdoors without the creature comforts of an hotel or guest house, or at least a solid, four-walled, roofed mountain hut between them and the elements. It is, in many ways, the natural reaction of ordinary, social, domesticated people.

Backpacking offers a chance to break away from these normal social constrictions, which in itself, if nothing else, makes a refreshing change from day-to-day living. But it has got to be more than that, it has got to be more than a mere rebellion from the norm. To "commune with nature" is a trite, overworked phrase which usually stimulates an impression that the user is a bit odd, but lie below a starlit sky with nothing more between you and the great outdoors than the flimsy shell of a bivvy bag, and listen to the muffled grunts of some nearby deer, watch a tiny squirrel, inquisitive, nervous, approach your inert body, or listen to the wind surf in the trees overhead. You will probably be closer to nature than at any time in your life.

Not everyone will agree, though. Many folk find it hard to relax in the outdoors. Beyond the friendly

If you are going to sleep outdoors, make sure that you plan your shelter. A simple tarpaulin, of coated nylon and fitted with grommets, can be rigged in any of the ways shown above. Trees make the best anchor points, but a stout walking staff will also do. When setting up your tarp, remember that the opening of your shelter should be out of the wind.

glare of their flickering candle lies a dark hostile world; an all-embracing menace lies out there in the shadows. Faint scuffles and grunts may be amplified into alarming proportions, and the sounds of tumbling water in the stream may mysteriously take on the drone of distant voices. To lie within the gossamer walls of a lightweight backpacking tent, and to listen to the wind shrieking and screaming over the hill beyond, waiting for its full mighty force to reach you with a bone-shaking shudder, takes a lot of courage.

But experience is a great teacher. When you know that your tiny tent is well pitched and sheltered and will not blow away; when you know that marauding squirrels, raccoons, or hedgehogs are incapable of harm; when you become sadly aware that man, God help us, by his very presence, puts fear and alarm into other creatures; then you realize that there is not much to worry about. The fear of the unknown is the most intangible of all our fears, and it is a fear that can quickly change to a love. The love of solitude; the love of the wild open spaces; the love of the smell of pine resin, and fresh coffee, and damp earth; the smell of a new day starting in the wilds.

By far the majority of my happy backpacking memories are of camp sites. The walking part of backpacking is often memorable too, but it is really a means to an end, which is the night out, either under the stars or in the tent. I also spend a lot of time on day trips. Living close to the mountains, I can charge off at a moment's notice and enjoy a day on the hill tops and be home in time for supper, but there is always something missing from days like this; there is always a tinge of regret as I leave the high beautiful places and trudge downwards in the darkening evening. It is as though I am leaving something behind. How much better it is to stay high; to find a small flat patch of grass to call home for the night. The finest part of the day, in my opinion, is early morning and the hour or so before darkness falls. On day trips, you invariably miss out on these magic moments. Far better to stay out and feel part of the wilderness as darkness closes in on you, spend the night comfortably ensconced in bivvy or tent, alone with your thoughts and dreams, or maybe with a good book, or perhaps even with a friend or loved one, and then awake early, refreshed, into a beautiful place.

There is something basic and elemental about setting up camp after a day on the trail. "Home is where I lay my hat" perhaps sums up the romanticism of the wanderer. To find a magnificent setting and to spend the night there is one of the most basic joys of backpacking, perhaps even of life itself. It is what man has done since time

(Below) A tarp is better than a tent for beach camping in hot weather. It works as a sun shelter rather than as a tent and it marks off living space, often a necessity on popular beaches. A tent would get filled with sand and can become unbearably hot.

A lightweight, hooped bivvy bag of Gore-Tex. As the inner volume is so low, any water vapour inside the bag is forced through the PTFE pores by body heat and then carried away by convection. Units like this, weighing only about 1.5 lb (700 g), are ideal for the backpacker who wants to keep weight to a minimum and yet still have a waterproof shelter at night. There is little thought of comfort, though, and you can do little more than lie down in this kind of shelter.

immemorial. And there is nothing in the rules to say you should spend only one night there. Close to my home is a mountain which I love dearly. It is not a particularly splendid mountain as mountains go, but one side of it has been scoured out by the action of glaciers into a great hollow, and in the bottom of that hollow is a tiny lake. In the eons since the glaciers did their work, heathers and mosses and lichens have grown, and small trees have taken root and flourished, small shapely pine trees which exude fragrant resin smells when the sun shines on them. Blueberries grow in abundance in high summer, and in the autumn, the air becomes alive with the sound of rutting deer stags. In winter, the snows lie deep here, but because it is well protected from the northern winds, it becomes a sanctuary to many of the deer who flee from the coarseness of the high tops. This magnificent setting has become my sanctuary, too. When things become hard, and I have problems to sort out, or if I feel that quiet meditation over a short period of time will improve my ability to be creative, I repair to this place in the hills. I pitch the tent below the pines close to the lake, allow myself to become enthralled again by the meditative quality of the place, and, relaxed, refreshed, I think. The great jumble of thoughts that have been bouncing about in my brain begin to take on a semblance of order, and by the time I have been there for a day and a night, I have things worked out.

Sometimes, I just forget the problems that have been worrying me, because there is something about the great outdoors which is greater and infinitely more important than the mediocre little anxieties that I think are problems. When I realize this, I can handle my problems in their proper perspective when I get home. Sometimes, when I have big problems like writing a book and not knowing what to put in it, I go to my place in the hills and work it out, maybe for three or four days at a time. I do not travel far in that time but spend a lot of the time on my back, propped against a rock, surveying the vast horizon. It is almost as though I come in contact with some Infinite Intelligence which then transmits the thought processes which eventually crack the problems. It is, I suppose, total relaxation, a refurbishment of the soul, and I, for one, revel in it. Because I spend nights in that place, either in a tent or sleeping in the open, I feel intimately towards it. I feel I know it almost as another home. Someone once wrote that to know a mountain, one has to sleep on it, and I could not

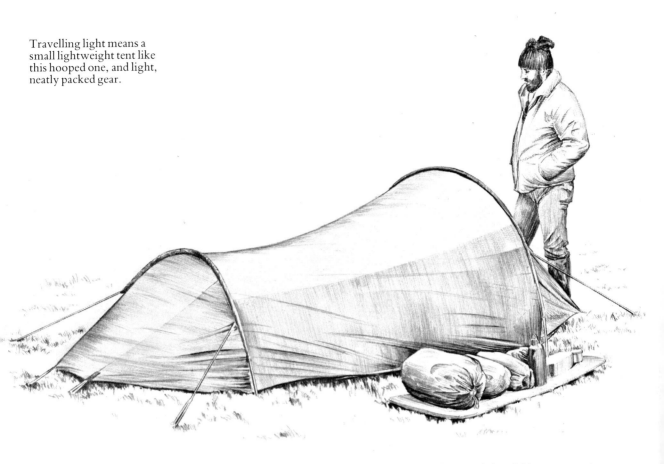

Travelling light means a small lightweight tent like this hooped one, and light, neatly packed gear.

agree more with that philosophy. To spend the full twenty-four-hour cycle in the outdoors gives a confidence in your ability to be at one with the environment. If you go home at night, or leave the hill for the comforts of an hotel, then you are merely a visitor.

I invariably use a tent at night, not because I do not like open-air sleeping, but because the climatic conditions in my part of the world are, to say the least, fickle. And there is nothing worse than waking up in the middle of the night with rain falling on you or insects eating you. Besides, a tent can become a sanctuary within a sanctuary. Inside a flimsy cocoon of nylon you create a micro-environment that is home, with the creature comforts of home: food, warmth, light, and amusement, usually in the form of good company or a good book. Quite often, usually when the weather is bad, I will cook in the bell end of the tent from the warmth and comfort of my sleeping-bag. A candle flickers its shadows on the tent walls and offers a warm orange glow to the inside of the tent. With the stove purring, and the aroma of hot food in the air, there is an atmosphere of sheer comfort that is impossible to describe unless you have experienced it. So many folk have told me that I

must be tough to endure such hardships as camping in the wild places for days and days on end. Toughness, my friends, does not come into it. Good reliable equipment, equipment which be-comes, over the years, like old friends, and the knowledge to use that equipment, are all that is necessary to enjoy lightweight camping.

Snow as a shelter

All is well spending the night under a tarp, plastic sheet, or even below the stars, in summer time, but backpacking without a tent in the depths of winter is simply asking for trouble. Having said that, you may well be caught out in winter weather without your tent, or you may head out with the deliberate intention of digging, and living in, a snow hole or a snow cave.

The insulating properties of snow are well known. Scientists at the University of Colorado have made comparisons between snow and down, in terms of insulation. In both, the insulating agent consists of millions of tiny, trapped dead-air pockets. In down, these dead-air pockets are formed between the particles of the feathers, and in snow exactly the same thing happens in the piling and

Digging a snow cave
Choose a snow bank that is high and deep.
1 Cut a large shaft, pulling out the snow blocks on a polythene bag.
2 Once well in, start widening the shaft. Cut out sleeping shelves at a higher level than the entrance hole (cold air sinks and warm air rises).
3 With the blocks you dug out and left to freeze, fill in the shaft entrance, leaving a low hole, just large enough to crawl through. Once inside the cave, stick an ice axe or a walking staff through the top of the entrance, to make a ventilation hole.

1

interlocking of the snow flakes. Small birds like the ptarmigan, and mammals like the blue hare, survive well in snowy winters, protected against the wind in the shelter of snow banks and snow holes.

A fresh layer of snow may hold between 60% and 90% air, depending upon its structure. Once snow has been on the ground for a time the shapes of the snowflakes change; the sharp points and edges disappear and the once beautiful flakes become globular masses. But much of the original air remains in the snow. The old snow may not hold as much air but what it does hold is more effectively

trapped, and the insulation qualities of the snow actually improves.

Once you dig a hole into this compact snow, you effectively insulate yourself in much the same way as you do when you crawl into a sleeping bag. The original temperature of the snow-trapped air is near the average air temperature at the time the snow fell, but very soon body heat and the heat from candles and stoves produce a considerable change inside the snow hole. Due to these heat sources, the air temperature inside the snow hole starts to rise towards freezing point. The temperature inside the

1

2

3

Making an igloo
Select your site well away from any potential avalanche slope. It requires a good deal of practice to build a solid igloo in reasonable time, and you ought to have an ice saw and a proper snow shovel.

So the igloo is not an emergency shelter, if, say, you need to get in out of a snow storm.

1 Mark out a circle and dig a shallow pit. The number of people sleeping in the igloo will decide its

size, but generally you can allow 10 ft (3 m) diameter for two or three people. With one person cutting out the blocks (16 × 32 × 10 inches thick—about 40 × 80 cm and 25 cm), the other can do the actual building. The blocks will

be stronger and easier to handle if they are allowed to stand on end and freeze for a while.

2 Stand inside the pit and place the blocks around the circumference in an inward-leaning spiral.

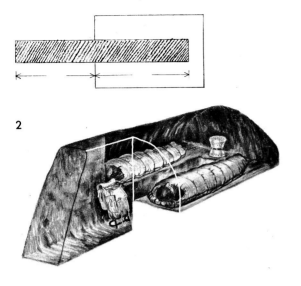

2

3

snow cave should be kept if at all possible below zero, so as to avoid drips from melting snow. Freezing point may not sound very attractive, but it is far superior to a warm, mushy, dripping snow cave at higher temperatures. To appreciate the comparative comfort of freezing level, stick your nose outside into the wind for a few moments, where the combination of breeze and cold make your snow hole feel like a centrally heated apartment... To make a real workmanlike job of creating a snow hole or cave, it is useful to have with you a small broad shovel, or even better, a snow saw. Few backpackers carry these implements, but if you go out with the direct intention of living in snow holes, then these two tools will make life a lot easier for you. Generally, backpackers will use an ice axe, pot lid, skis, ski poles, their hands and feet, and anything else suitable to build emergency snow holes.

IGLOOS

The pure igloo can take a lot of time to build and requires the use of a shovel and snow saw. It offers in the end, though, a solid, structurally sound

4

5

6

3 Build gradually upward, remembering to camber the blocks so that they lean inward.

4 Lower the final block, the keystone in the roof, gently into position. Cut out a doorway in the cross-wind side, to avoid being drifted up by the snow.

5 Smooth off the walls, plastering them with snow to seal the crevices.

6 Build a short entrance tunnel. Poke out a couple of ventilation holes in the roof. Once inside the igloo, you can go ahead and luxuriate, building sleeping benches and cooking areas to your heart's content.

shelter which will remain standing for a long time, even in a thaw. The problem with igloo building is that the snow must have the right consistency. New unconsolidated snow which is packed and allowed to harden is ideal, but this takes a lot of time. Wet snow can be rolled into great snowballs, and then cut into block shapes, but even a small igloo takes a lot of snowballs, and it is very hard work. Ideally, you need snow which is hard enough to take your weight when standing on it without snow shoes or skis. The snow should have the same consistency throughout the block and not just be crusted on top.

LIVING IN SNOW

Sleep in a dry sleeping-bag, with dry clothes on. It is the only way you will keep warm at night. Once your clothes or sleeping-bag become wet, there is every chance they will freeze. When you enter your shelter, strip off your damp clothes, and put them into a plastic bag or stuff sack, and then get into your sleeping-bag.

Digging a snow shelter is usually hard, sweaty work. Before you start digging, strip off to the very minimum you will need for protection, so that only the minimum of clothing will get wet from perspiration.

Make sure that you have adequate ventilation in the hole or igloo. Failure to do so could result in death from anoxia, lack of oxygen. Bring everything inside the snow hole with you, especially your digging implements. The shelter entrance may well drift over and you will want to get out again. If you leave the snow hole for any time, mark it well so that you can find it again, and leave your digging implements outside. You may have to dig your way in again. Bring boots and clothing up on the sleeping bench beside you. Put them in a stuff sack and use it as a pillow. Don't leave them on the floor, where they could freeze to the ground.

As in a tent, brush off all the snow from your clothing before you enter the shelter. If you do not, the snow will melt once it meets the warmer temperatures inside the snow hole. Avoid food which takes a lot of simmering or boiling. Water vapour given off from the pot will cause condensation to form and will dampen your sleeping-bag and clothing.

A candle in the snow hole or igloo is better than a flashlight or lantern. One single candle can illuminate a whole cave, for the snow reflects off the millions of snow crystals and gives an effect like Father Christmas's Grotto.

Put plenty of insulation between the snow and the sleeping-bag. Don't lie directly on top of a plastic bag or you will most likely slip off your sleeping bench during the night. Always leave a light burning if you have to get out of the shelter during the night, as this may be the only indication you will have of where your shelter is. It is also a good idea to mark the outside top of the snow hole with some form of marker, even in daytime.

Chap. 5

CAMPING EQUIPMENT

The tent

For comfort, privacy, protection and shelter, there is nothing better than a well-designed, lightweight, stable tent. There is no item of backpacking equipment that has metamorphosed so much in recent years into an apparently endless stream of shapes and designs, as the lightweight tent. The traditional and familiar ridge tent is still a popular breed, but in the constant search for more internal volume for less weight, tent designers have produced space-age designs using hoops and fibreglass wands instead of rigid aluminium poles, and breathable/waterproof Gore-Tex instead of proofed nylon which requires two skins, a flysheet and an inner tent, to combat the scourge of condensation.

With such an incredible array of shapes and sizes, not to mention materials, available to the novice backpacker today, how do we go about choosing what we really need to give us those factors of comfort, protection, and light weight?

Weight in a tent is a difficult thing to categorize. An 8-lb (3.6 kg) model, with enough room to take three backpackers, will, if you habitually travel with two other companions, be effectively lighter than a one-person tent that is half that weight. By sharing the weight of the tent, one person for example taking the poles and pegs, another the flysheet, and the other the inner tent, you drastically cut down the weight of tent per person. But if you do not travel with companions, that tent will weigh heavily on your shoulders. On the other hand, if you have a one-person tent, you may want to share it occasionally with a friend. If it is a true one-person tent, that friend will have to be a very close one, and you will not have much room for modesty.

Generally speaking, tents that are advertised as one-person units are rarely big enough internally for a dog. Two-person tents are usually comfortable for one, and three-person tents offer comfortable living space for two. Bear this in mind when you are choosing what tent to buy. Manufacturers tend, generally speaking, to skimp on sizings, to both cut the cost of the manufactured unit and to cut down on the weight of the finished product, so that that ultra-lightweight model you plan to buy may just be a bit on the small side, especially if you are planning on having company. Remember too, if you plan to spend your backpacking nights in a small lightweight tent, that you may want to camp during the winter. It is amazing how quickly a small, low-internal-volume tent takes on the appearance of a coffin during the long slow hours of winter darkness. You become cramped, claustrophobic, and very uncomfortable, and it is then that you wish you had bought something with a bit more space to move around in.

In deciding on what sort of tent you want, consider whether you are only a summer backpacker, camping at low levels for most of the time, or do you intend camping in the mountains, maybe in the depths of winter? A tent with a single pole at the front and one at the rear, weighing 3.5 lb (1.5 kg), and made of some flimsy proofed nylon may well give sufficient protection and shelter during the balmy nights of spring and summer, but high-level, and more importantly, winter backpacking calls for A-poles, or a geodesic dome design, strong stitching, and a little more basic weight to withstand the stress of windy weather, storms, and the weight of fallen snow.

TENT CONSTRUCTION

The construction of the tent is important, especially in high-level tents and tents that are to be used in

Tents
Recent tent design has aimed at decreased weight, increased internal volume, and greater stability.

(Above) Geodesic dome tents have almost 50% more internal volume than A-frame tents with the same floor space. The bell end in the larger picture should be standard on all tents.

(Right) This A-pole ridge tent has three external frames and is robust enough for mountain backpacking.

(Right) A one-pole pyramid tent for the most rigorous conditions, with a polycotton inner tent and an Aluflex outer tent, a storm mat all round, and a wind-sheltered opening that can be raised on poles, where gear and clothes can be freed from snow before you enter the tent itself.

(Centre) One of the advantages of the hooped tunnel tent is that even larger versions can be moved by one person.

Here we show a four-man tent with treble hoops.

(Left) A lightweight tunnel tent for one—at most two—backpackers.

Dome-tent construction

A The poles *(1)* in the pole sleeves *(2)* hold the tent in tension and create a dead-air space between the tent and the flysheet (not shown here).

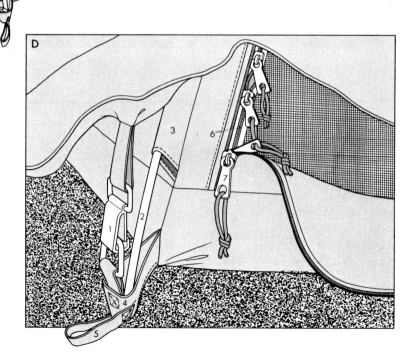

B The flysheet in position. It has bell ends at either end for cooking and storage. This means that the tent can be cross-ventilated. *(1)* Storm guy. *(2)* Extra rings and neoprene shock cords for additional anchorage in bad weather.
C Plan of tent showing line of poles and the bell ends.
D Detail of tent, with flysheet raised to show the nylon snap clips *(1)* that attach the flysheet to the tent. *(2)* Pole. *(3)* Pole sleeve. *(4)* Pole pocket. *(5)* Finger pull. *(6)* Double zip on mosquito door. *(7)* Double zip on outer door.

winter. Luckily, most of the points can be checked in the store before buying.

Seams

For maximum strength, the best method of sewing seams is the flat, lap-felled method. The fabric edges fold around each other and are sewn together. Simple seams will not withstand the stress and strain of tent usage as much as do these felled seams, and they are next to useless in tents which will be under considerable stress, e.g. in snow, in high winds, or from heavy usage.

Stitching

Stitching should be evenly spaced, uniform in tension, and run straight along the entire seam length, with preferably three to four stitches per cm (about seven to nine stitches per inch).

Lock-stitching is more durable and less likely to unravel than chain-stitching and has the added advantage of not unravelling should one of the threads break, unlike chain-stitching. Look out for crooked stitching, variations in tightness, and puckered seams, as these are all potential weak spots. Loose ends where the stitching stops and uncaught fabric edges are sure signs of sloppy workmanship. Seams that end without backstitching are another warning of potential failure points. Awkward sewing areas, like the ends of zips and in tight corners, should be checked carefully, as these are the likely areas for bad workmanship.

Stress point reinforcement

Places to check for reinforcement are seam junctions, apexes, pole-sleeve ends, and points where grommets, peg loops, and straps attach. Peg loops and straps are often bar-tacked for additional strength. The best type of reinforcement is an extra piece of nylon, or even leather, added to the relevant area of the tent, with straps and loops sewn between the double thickness. Stitching at reinforcement points should be checked and is critical, as a weak thread here could have serious consequences in the wilds.

DOME TENTS

With the recent wave of new materials and technology in outdoor-gear manufacture, it was only a matter of time before the tent-design gurus of the world began paying attention to what Buckminster Fuller said way back in the 'sixties. Fuller was an architect and inventor, one of the greatest of this century, and it was he who first

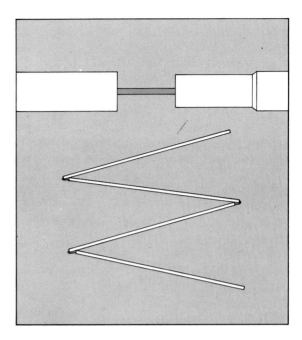

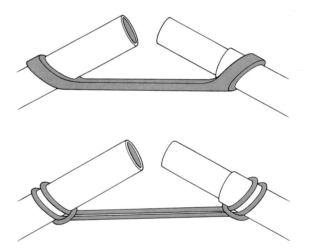

The long poles used in dome tents and hoop tents come in two types, shock-corded and non-shock-corded. The former **(top)** have a length of elasticated material running through the hollow core of the pole, making pole assembly quick and simple. You cannot lose a section, and breaking down for packing is easy.

(Centre) Non-shock-corded poles are normally solid fibreglass. By tying elasticated material with this simple knot, you can link the poles permanently.

97

This particular tent is simple to erect, as its inner and outer tents are joined. The tent is laid on the ground and the aluminium poles are threaded through the pole sleeves on the outer tent.

The poles are bent and the ends are fitted into grommets in shock cords fitted to the four corners of the tent.

The tent can now be moved as a unit to the desired position.

With the tent in position, the bell end can be erected and, if necessary, the storm guys put up. If the weather is calm, guys are not necessary, as the tent is self-supporting.

Low-level lightweight tents

A The most basic is the single-pole ridge tent. A separate flysheet over an inner tent helps reduce condensation by allowing the vapour from body heat and cooking to permeate the breathable though showerproof inner tent. The airflow between flysheet and the inner tent should carry away the vapour.

The square-ended ridge tent (**B**) and the transverse ridge tent (**C**) are variations on the theme of the basic ridge tent.

D The double A-pole design provides the strength and stability necessary in the mountain backpacking tent.

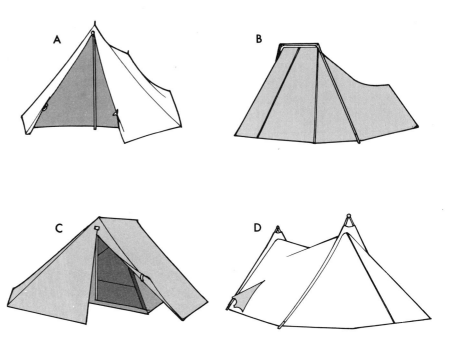

E This single A-pole tent is strengthened by a pole at the back. Not quite up to mountain standards.

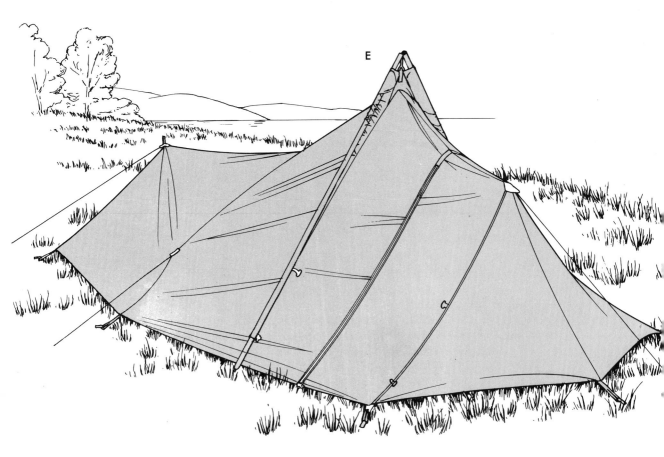

began working out design concepts based on the geodesic principle. With recent advances in flexible, tubular pole materials such as fibreglass and aluminium alloys, the geodesic tent is now a reality rather than a drawing-board dream.

The big advantages of dome tents are increased living space and the fact that they are highly efficient shapes for shedding wind and rain. With no corners, sharp edges, or flat surfaces, dome-shaped designs offer a smooth airfoil to the wind. Another advantage to bear in mind is the smaller surface-to-volume ratio. This can be a fairly important factor for those interested in cold-weather camping; the smaller the tent surface, the less heat it will radiate. Less actual tent material is required compared to traditional A-frame tents, although it must be said that the reduced weight in material is more than offset by the increased weight of the elaborate systems of poles which are necessary to keep a dome tent upright and erect.

But what of the disadvantages of dome tents? When I think of the problems I have encountered at one time or another when testing dome tents, it strikes me that the most frequent complaint concerns poles. Whether it is the increased weight of the poles, the plumber's nightmare of threading the sections together, the necessity of careful man-oeuvring of the connected wands through seemingly yards of sleeved tent material, or the damage which can be inflicted on poles through innocent abuse, dome-tent poles have come out tops on the list of disadvantages.

Perhaps inexperience causes us to take longer to erect dome tents than more traditional designs, but it seems that erecting dome tents takes a bit of getting used to. Weight, too, is a disadvantage of domes. If you habitually share your tent with someone, then the weight of the tent is not so much of a problem. By sharing the weight, loads can be kept fairly low, though dome tents usually are heavier than traditional ridge tents. Dome tents are generally more expensive, too.

There seems to be a growing controversy over which method of pole assembly is best suited to dome tents. Many argue that there is no such thing as a truly self-supporting tent, that is, a tent which has no guy lines for extra anchorage, while others claim that the pole interaction of the geodesic design gives a more rigid structure to resist strong winds.

The geodesic design utilizes very sophisticated concepts whereby the poles follow the arcs of great circles; a great circle being the shortest distance between two points on a curved surface. By cross-ing the tent poles to form polygons whose outward thrusts are balanced by equalizing compression factors, a virtually distortion-free structure is produced. That sounds complicated, but in effect it is simple. The pole structure of the geodesic design is such that wind loading is distributed over the entire pole system, resulting in the elimination of flapping tent materials. Such a tendency is not only noisy and disturbs sleep but it can weaken the tent fabric and stitching. The pole structure also effectively cuts down the actual length of unsupported pole, reducing the possibility of distortion in windy weather.

By using a four-pole geodesic design, rigidity of the structure is greatly increased. This is due to the fact that all the poles are in outward tension and, at the same time, compressed by the pegged-out flysheet; the vector forces (directional forces) are then balanced, and this greatly aids stability.

The cross-over pole design is possibly inferior unless used on a single-skin design construction. Because of the long lengths of unsupported poles in the cross-over pole design, the tent will deform badly in wind, requiring considerable guying to hold it stable in windy conditions. In addition to this problem, as the tent deforms to sideways pressure, there is a great risk of the flysheet touching the inner tent, and wetting it with condensation. In short, crossover-pole systems work on small tents that are of single-skin designs, like Gore-Tex fabric tents, but for really effective stability in rough weather, you should consider a four-pole geodesic design. Having said this, medium-sized crossover pole designs do not distort too badly in side winds, and this can be alleviated almost totally by guying the poles firmly to the ground.

Pole systems for dome tents must be pliable and easily curved, but not so easily curved that they will distort badly under pressure. I have tested, in the past, very cheap alloy poles which distort so easily that they maintain their curved shape even when not under tension. Pultrued (reinforced by a special method) fibreglass poles are much better, but they suffer from the problem of being solid, so they cannot be shock corded together.

Fibreglass pole sections are also susceptible to very cold weather and can easily crack in sub-zero temperatures. Fibreglass poles are relatively cheap, though, and bring dome tents within the price range of most campers. The best dome-tent poles are American—70/75T9 anodized aluminium alloy. These poles are all shock-corded together, have ferruled close-fit joints, and are usually of the same size to alleviate sorting problems. This type of pole is generally used in the more expensive dome-tent models.

As designs move continually towards free-standing domes, the search for stronger, lighter, yet more resilient poles continues. Some manufacturers are experimenting with all sorts of weird materials: graphite epoxy, titanium, boron fibreglass and even, it is claimed, ground sapphire… Fabrics, too, are constantly being improved, and very light-weight, yet strong, nylons are now being used in various tent-makers, prototypes.

TIPS ON CHOOSING YOUR TENT

First of all, define your needs. Are you a year-round camper? Do you need a tent which will have to stand up to the rigours of high-altitude camping, or are you a weekend summer-camper only? Are you a backpacker, cyclist, canoe tourer, or solo traveller whose major concern is minimal weight, or do you require room for your friends, your dog, or your family? How much do you have to spend? Remember that a good tent is a good investment and should last a long time. An expensive tent does not necessarily mean it is a good one, and a cheap

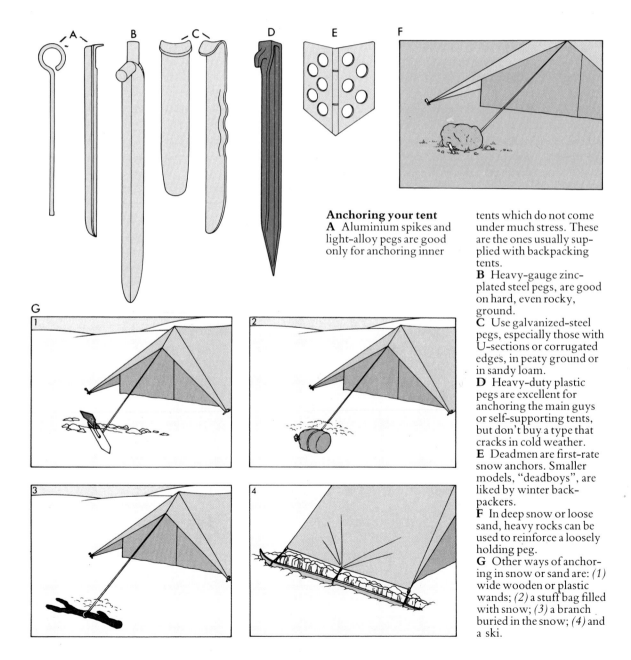

Anchoring your tent
A Aluminium spikes and light-alloy pegs are good only for anchoring inner tents which do not come under much stress. These are the ones usually supplied with backpacking tents.
B Heavy-gauge zinc-plated steel pegs, are good on hard, even rocky, ground.
C Use galvanized-steel pegs, especially those with U-sections or corrugated edges, in peaty ground or in sandy loam.
D Heavy-duty plastic pegs are excellent for anchoring the main guys or self-supporting tents, but don't buy a type that cracks in cold weather.
E Deadmen are first-rate snow anchors. Smaller models, "deadboys", are liked by winter back-packers.
F In deep snow or loose sand, heavy rocks can be used to reinforce a loosely holding peg.
G Other ways of anchor-ing in snow or sand are: *(1)* wide wooden or plastic wands; *(2)* a stuff bag filled with snow; *(3)* a branch buried in the snow; *(4)* and a ski.

one does not always mean it is inferior. Ask yourself these questions, then go to a reputable store and ask more. By spending some time chewing over the various problems, types, and models, you will in all probability make a wise choice in the end: the tent best-suited to your particular needs.

GORE-TEX FABRIC TENTS

As most backpackers are by now aware, Gore-Tex fabric is a .001-inch (.0025 cm) thick Teflon-like plastic film with 9 billion pores per sq in (1.4 billion per sq cm). The pores are some 20,000 times smaller than a water droplet, preventing rain or dew from percolating through the material. The pores, however, are more than 700 times larger than water-vapour molecules, which when conditions are right, will pass right through the fabric.

Because Gore-Tex fabric itself is so thin, it must be bonded to another fabric for durability; in tents, it is usually laminated to ripstop nylon. The resulting laminate usually has an overall weight of 2.6 oz per sq yard (67.8 grams per sq m), which makes it slightly heavier than the standard ripstop nylon used in traditional-material tents. Where Gore-Tex fabric does score well in tent design is in the fact that it does not need a flysheet. This can save anything up to 2 lb (1 kg) or more on the total tent weight.

Gore-Tex fabric tents are used normally without vents, because the fabric works best in a totally closed unit. Body heat warms the air and creates inside the tent a slightly higher vapour pressure which pushes water vapour out through the miniscule Gore-Tex pores. If a door is left open, or if there is an air vent, interior pressure remains about the same as the outside, and moisture will condense if the surface of the fabric is cool enough – just like on proofed nylon. Bearing this in mind, it seems that cold weather can pose two special problems for Gore-Tex fabric tents. First of all, if you are bundled up in a thick sleeping bag, your radiated body heat is often insufficient to warm the air inside the tent. The result is usually a frosting up of the interior of the tent. Secondly, it has been felt that there is the distinct possibility of carbon-monoxide poisoning if you cook inside a *closed* Gore-Tex fabric tent. If it is sealed tight in an attempt to create enough vapour pressure to get rid of the steam, carbon monoxide produced by the burning stove can build up to dangerous proportions. So, if you want to cook inside a Gore-Tex fabric tent, make sure there is adequate air-flow ventilation. If you still get a problem with steam inside the tent, despite having the doors open, move on outside and cook. You must also realize that it is dangerous to burn a stove, especially a petrol stove, inside any sealed tent, Gore-Tex or not, but if you impress on people that to work effectively in winter, a Gore-Tex fabric tent must be sealed for maximum efficiency, someone, somewhere, will end up with carbon-monoxide poisoning.

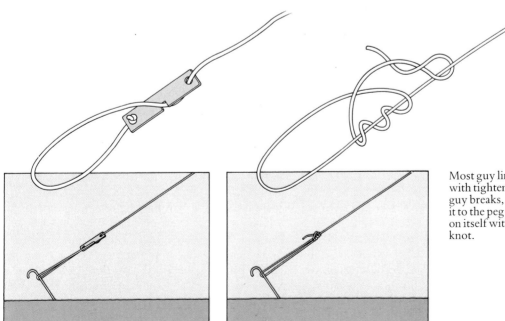

Most guy lines are fitted with tighteners, but if your guy breaks, you can secure it to the peg by tying it back on itself with this sliding knot.

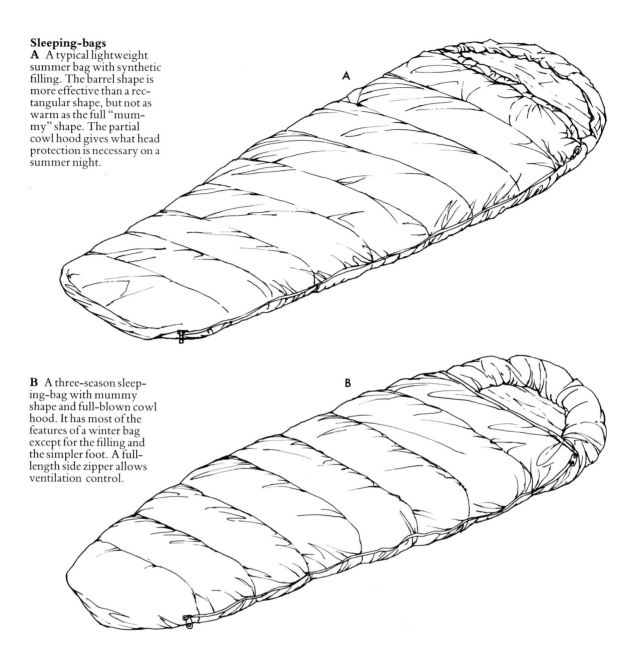

Sleeping-bags
A A typical lightweight summer bag with synthetic filling. The barrel shape is more effective than a rectangular shape, but not as warm as the full "mummy" shape. The partial cowl hood gives what head protection is necessary on a summer night.

B A three-season sleeping-bag with mummy shape and full-blown cowl hood. It has most of the features of a winter bag except for the filling and the simpler foot. A full-length side zipper allows ventilation control.

PEGS

A tent is only as good as the anchors which hold it to the ground. Tent performance is usually poorer when the pegging conditions are poor, so if you are pitched in sand, snow, or very soft earth, you may well find that the pegs yield to the pressure of the taut guylines, especially if it is windy. This in turn allows the tent fabric to lose its tautness and develop slack. Self-supporting tents, in many ways, get around this problem, but they still need to be anchored to the ground. When you are inside the tent, your body weight does this quite effectively, but tents also need to stay put when no one is inside.

Check that the peg loops on the tent are wide enough to take a large variety of peg sizes. It is surprising how many tents have loops only big enough to take the smallest size peg. Which brings us to the question of the pegs supplied with tents. In an effort to cut the cost and weight of tents, many manufacturers only supply lightweight cheap pegs, which, in a great many cases, are totally inadequate. I have always felt that there is a case for manufacturers not supplying pegs, but leaving the choice up to the buyer. It pays dividends to have a wide variety of pegs for different ground conditions, and it is also wise, despite the extra weight, to carry a few extra pegs.

C The complete four-season sleeping-bag, with slant-wall construction, a full cowl hood, and a boxed foot which gives the feet more room and increased insulation.

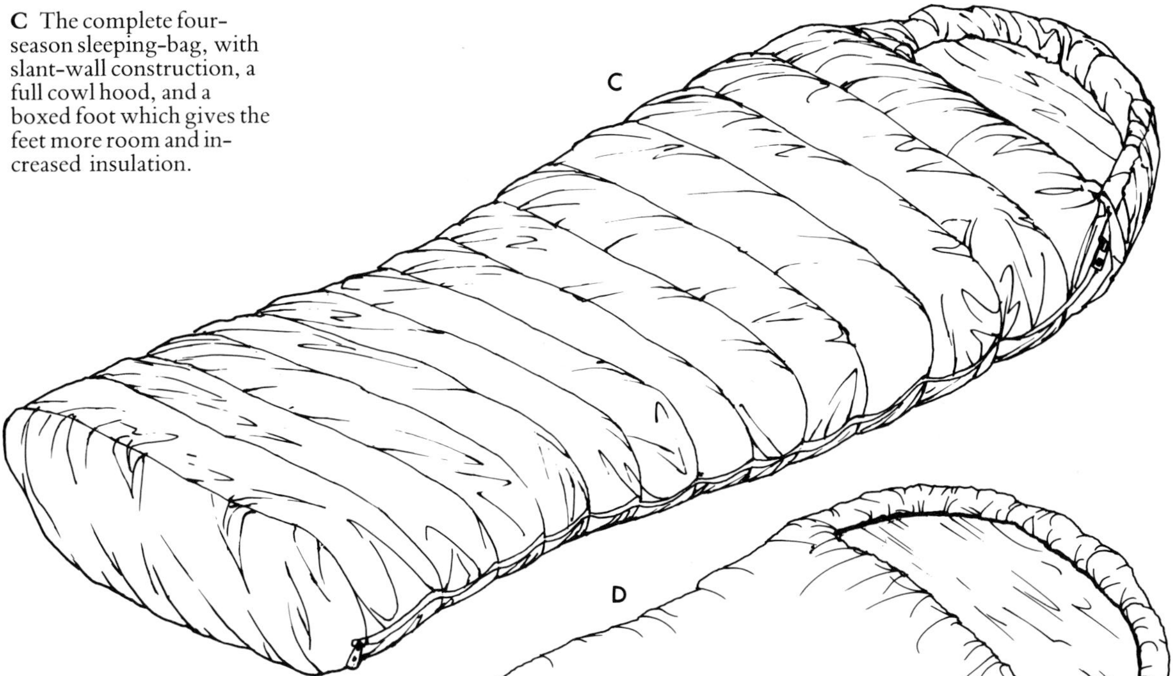

C

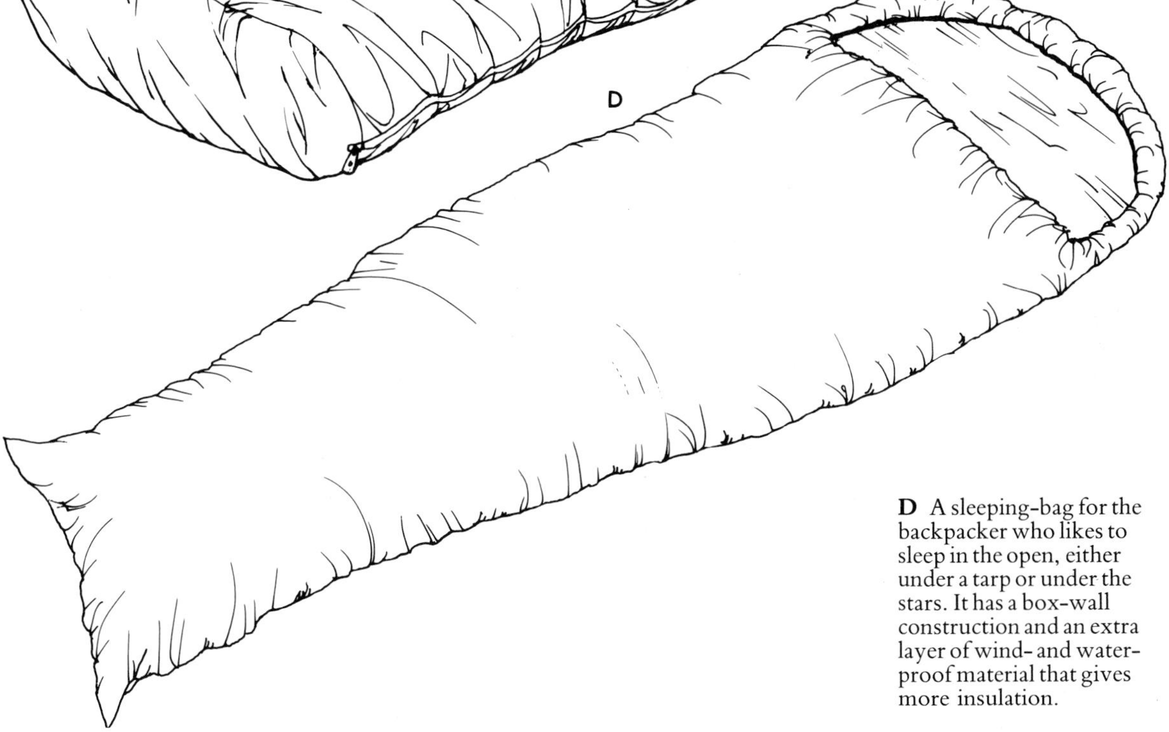

D

D A sleeping-bag for the backpacker who likes to sleep in the open, either under a tarp or under the stars. It has a box-wall construction and an extra layer of wind- and water-proof material that gives more insulation.

TENT CARE

Despite the fact that most modern backpacking tents are made from non-corroding nylons, never store your tent away wet. The threads which hold the tent together may possibly be made from cotton, and if they rot, the whole unit will simply fall apart.

Try and maintain your tent in good condition. Sponge dirty marks from it whenever you finish a trip, especially the inner tent which can soil very easily. Make sure that the tent is clean and dry before you pack it away in the off-season. Carry a small repair kit with you, of the type which can be purchased from most backpacking stores. If you

pitch on sharp and stony ground, put something under the groundsheet to protect it, and never place your stove on the groundsheet itself; it will probably melt it. Pitch your tent before you go off on your trip, and check that everything is in good condition, that you have the correct amount of pegs, and that all the guy lines are complete and unknotted. Do the same when you return home.

Sleeping-bags

When we crawl into our tent at night, and slip our body inside a sleeping-bag, we enter another world. No matter what the weather conditions are outside, we can now create our own micro-climate; we are safe and warm; we are physically, and usually mentally, cut off not only from the world outside, but from our companions too. Sleep, the great restorer, embraces us.

But only if we are warm and comfortable.

At night, we are at our most defenseless. We are normally capable of taking an astonishing amount of punishment in the course of a day; we may be snowed on, rained on, fogged in, blown about, frazzled by a merciless sun. We may physically drain our bodies of energy, we may do without the recommended amount of food and water, we may treat our bodies cruelly. And yet, we can still smile. We know damned well that in a few weeks time we will look back on the experience from the confines of our everyday routine and wish that once again, we were out there in the wild places, accepting whatever nature chooses to throw at us. But at night, discomfort cannot be accepted so graciously. Wet and cold cannot be tolerated at night, when sleep should be taking us by the hand and soothing the weary muscles. Sleepless nights drain us of everything, not the least being enthusiasm, and without that enthusiasm, the urge to stay in the outdoors dissipates like steam from a kettle.

Happily, man has evolved several marvellous materials which will keep him warm in the most inhospitable of environments, and amazingly, this can be done with a minimum of weight and bulk. Mountaineers in the Arctic or on Everest wrap themselves in a cocoon of nylon and goose down, a cocoon which weighs little more than 4 to 5 lb (about 2 kg) in weight. We backpackers can head off in winter with a package which weighs little more than a kilo and is no larger than a loaf of bread; and that package will become our closest friend.

But how can such a slight bundle of feather and nylon keep us warm in sub-zero conditions? Well, man is constantly producing heat, like a radiator that never switches off, and to remain comfortable, he has to lose body heat at the same rate that he is producing it; this is called heat balance. During an active day, this is done by removing some clothing if it is too hot, or putting some clothing on if it is chilly. At night, when he wants to sleep, he is inactive and is not producing a lot of heat. The heat that is produced, however, is precious and must be captured by some form of insulating barrier. The sleeping-bag makes an admirable one.

The main function of a sleeping-bag is to retain body temperature by ensuring that heat is not lost faster than it is generated. The body also breathes

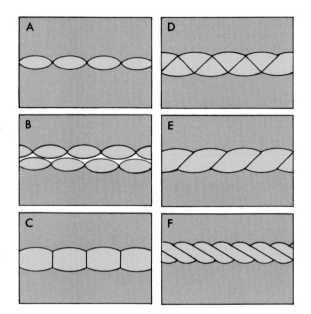

Sleeping-bag construction

A sleeping-bag consists of two fabric shells with the filling in between. To keep the filling evenly distributed and in place, the covers are stitched together. The method of stitching is all-important to the bag's insulating qualities.

A Simple quilting. Don't buy a sleeping-bag with simple quilting. The filling is compressed so much at the seams that there is no air trapped there, and the insulation value is practically nil.

B Double quilting consists of two simple quilts put together with the seams offset to eliminate the cold spots at the simple quilt's seams. This construction is, obviously, double the weight and, depending on the filler, could be too heavy for backpacking use.

C The box-wall construction has a vertical baffle that forms a wall between the inner and the outer shell and so gives the bag a uniform thickness throughout its length.

D The slanted-wall construction can take more

filling than can the box-wall construction, and is therefore warmer and more expensive. It is used mostly in down-filled winter bags.

E The overlapping-tube, or V-baffle, construction. Very efficient, but heavyweight and expensive.

F The sandwiched-batt construction eliminates the cold-spot problem but makes a fairly heavy bag.

out water vapour and for comfort to be maintained this must be allowed to escape without condensing inside the sleeping bag.

The best insulating medium is warm, still, dry air. Practicalities, however, rule out a simple cocoon of air. What we require is a medium which will trap the air, allow it to be warmed by our body heat, and stop it moving around to prevent it being cooled by convection. Other considerations are important, too. We need an insulator which is lightweight, and which compresses well so that it is not bulky.

FILLINGS

Down, fibre pile, and synthetic fillings such as Polarguard, Hollowfil, and Quallofil, are all excellent as insulators. When these fillings are used in a well-designed sleeping-bag, they not only provide a thick layer which is over 95% air, but they also keep the air still.

(Left) A layer of air is the best barrier to loss of heat by conduction. But if the space for the air is too big, the air moves around in it and convection currents carry the heat away.

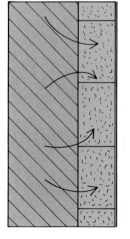

(Right) If the space is filled with, say, down, then the air is trapped by the down and is kept as still as possible.

Down

In dry conditions, down is by far the finest sleeping-bag insulator in the world. Nothing that is made by modern man has all its qualities of loft, compressibility and lasting resilience. It will keep you warm for less weight and bulk than any other insulating material.

Eiderdown The finest sleeping-bag filling that is available to man. Unfortunately, it has been virtually unobtainable since about 1940. It has been claimed that to make a sleeping bag from eiderdown today would cost in excess of $2,000 or about £1,000.

Goosedown The best current sleeping-bag insulator. With much of the world's supply of goosedown coming from China, the market fluctuates madly. The ordinary backpacker with not so much money to spend on camping equipment will find goosedown to be exorbitantly expensive, but it makes superlative sleeping-bags. It gives higher loft when open and less bulk when packed than any other material. The best quality available will contain an average of 95% down overall with not less than 85% at any one point. The rest of the filling will be made up of small curled feathers which cannot be separated from the down.

Duckdown At its very best, duckdown is only marginally inferior to goosedown. More commonly available than goosedown, there is also a wider range in quality. New down is best, but occasionally this is mixed with re-cycled down or cleaned, used down. Such fillings will, of course, be cheaper but inferior to all new down fillings.

Duckdown/feather mixtures At best, these will contain only about 50% down, and the quality of the feathers will vary significantly. Insulation is poorer than with pure down, and weight is increased. You will find these down-and-feather mixtures in the cheaper ranges of sleeping bags, but less so nowadays than several years ago, since the vast majority of sleeping-bag manufacturers are now using synthetics.

Fibre pile

The use of fibre pile for sleeping-bags, but even more so in sleeping-bag liners, has become more popular in recent years. Fibre pile has some unique qualities. It is extremely comfortable against the skin, is warm for its thickness, and is an unrivalled performer in wet conditions. It is also a good underbody insulator, and it has a long lifespan. Unfortunately, fibre-pile sleeping-bags are both heavy and bulky, and to achieve the minimum of weight and bulk, the manufacturers tend to cut them rather slim-fitting, which makes for rather claustrophobic sleeping. Far more successful are the lightweight fibre-pile sleeping-bag liners which can be used on their own in the balmy nights of summer, or with another sleeping-bag in winter to defeat the coldest of nights.

Synthetics

Most of these are of polyester fibre of one quality or another. The currently popular fillings are Polarguard, Hollowfil, and Quallofill. None of these synthetic fillings, despite the claims of manufacturers, are nearly as warm as down, and they are much heavier and bulkier. A good selling point, though, is that synthetic fillings do not lose much of their insulation when wet or damp, unlike down which clumps together and becomes virtually useless.

Until fairly recently, all commercially successful fillings were produced in batt form. Now, the "blown" synthetic filling has appeared and offers some very real advantages.

Batt form This method entails assembling short (normally) staple fibres into a controlled width and thickness, and then spraying with a resin to maintain the shape. The batt is then covered on both sides with appropriate fabric which is stitched through to form a quilted sandwich. A single layer is often used for lightweight models, but this tends to give rise to cold spots. Two offset layers are normally used to defeat this problem. The main advantage of this method is the stability of the filling—it cannot move about. Its chief drawbacks are weight, and the fact that however resilient the filling, it cannot loft beyond the limits set out by the proximity of the nearest stitch line.

Blown-filled bags These use the straight- or slant-walled baffle systems to give the excellent distribution and loft associated with down bags. There are no cold spots as in single-quilted bags, and the construction is lighter than in double layering. Boxes can be either lengthwise or widthwise—widthwise is best as it reduces the room available for movement. Care has to be taken with blown filling to ensure that the bag has sufficient filling to eliminate any tendency to shift away from the baffles. For this reason this method is best suited to three- and four-season bags.

Radiant barrier

This is a relatively new concept in sleeping-bags and has been proved to increase the performance of a

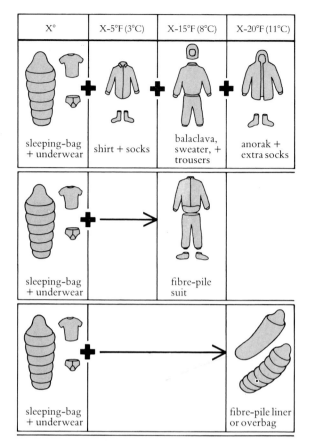

If you have a lightweight sleeping-bag suitable for summer and the warmer spring and autumn nights, you can extend its range by wearing extra clothing. As the table shows, however, a fibre-pile liner or an overbag can increase your bag's range by as much as 20°F (11°C).

sleeping-bag weight for weight by about 20%. In practice, the radiant barrier is used to reduce the weight and bulk by 20% for the same level of performance. This places the radiant-barrier sleeping-bag somewhere between down and normal synthetic bags for weight/bulk/warmth ratio. Moreover, the radiant-barrier sleeping-bag has the wet-performance advantage of synthetics. It achieves these savings by retaining all the heat normally lost by radiation—non-radiant bags cut down on heat loss by conduction and convection only. So the combination of radiant barrier and synthetic filling works on three main elements of heat loss rather than two.

SHELL MATERIALS

Shell materials must not leak, must be tough, non-rotting, lightweight, and permeable to allow water vapour from the body to pass through to the outside air. It must also be draught proof and the inner shell should feel comfortable against the skin. The most common materials are:

2 oz nylon: plain, sturdy, cheap, with most of the required qualities for inner and outer shells.

2 oz Ripstop nylon: similar but far tougher. Good for outer shells.

Nylon taffeta: 1.5 oz or less. Comfortable, very lightweight and good for inner shells too.

Cotton: comfortable but heavy. Used mainly for inners and needs considerable care.

Polycotton: comfortable but heavy. Tougher than cotton for inners.

Gore-Tex: a specialist material that makes the outer shell completely waterproof yet allows it to breathe. Excellent for expedition bags and for covering down-filled bags, which are susceptible to poor performance when wet. It is often used as a separate sleeping-bag cover.

GENERAL DESIGN FEATURES

Size and Shape Some bags have specific weights for specific reasons. Backpacking bags, for example, are slim fitting to save weight. In general, you should be able to pull the hood up without your feet being pressed up hard against the bottom of the bag. Remember too, that there should be room inside the bag to allow you to wear some extra clothes if necessary. Any more internal space than this is a waste of weight and thermal efficiency.

Zips Bags with side zips can be opened for easy entry and for allowing some cool air in on warm nights. Full-length double-ended zips allow bags to be zipped together to make double bags.

Drawbacks, of course, are additional weight and something extra to break... Make certain, though, that the zipper has an adequate tube of insulation behind it to seal off the cold and draughts.

Stitching Stitch size is important to the life of the bag. Look for a minimum of 8 stitches per inch (three per cm) and preferably ten (four) on both down and synthetic bags. Also look out for run backs (loose stitches) at the end of quilt lines on synthetics.

CHOOSING YOUR SLEEPING-BAG

Decide what kind of camping you will be doing most of the time, then decide what class of bag you will need. Don't make your decision by the most extreme camping you are likely to do, especially if it will only be once or twice a year. Combination bags, or even extra clothing can easily make up the difference on these rare occasions. Decide what matters most to you: weight? bulk? wet perform-ance? length of life? easy care? or price?

MAKE THE MOST OF YOUR SLEEPING-BAG

Think about how you will use your sleeping-bag and try and get the very best performance from it. Try and find shelter; sleep in a tent or in any shelter you can find that reduces the wind. Remember that the bare breast of Mother Nature is a cold bosom indeed, and you will need some form of ground insulation to stop your body warmth draining away. Dry any moisture out of your bag at the first opportunity. This is especially important with down. Wash your sleeping-bag occasionally (about once a year for normal use), carefully following the recommended instructions, and always store down and synthetic bags uncompressed.

INSULATION MATS

When we lay our body down to rest at night, the parts of the sleeping-bag underneath us are compressed, so that in effect all there is between you and the ground is some crushed feathers or synthetic filling plus some very thin nylon. One of the secrets of sleeping warm is insulation from the ground. We need a mattress or a sleeping pad. There are three basic types: open-cell foam, closed-cell foam, and air beds. Air beds can be a problem. Although they are reasonably thick, the air that is trapped inside is not still air. Your body warmth heats the air at the top of the mattress, but the warm air comes into contact with the cold ground and it loses heat. On top of that, air beds are liable to puncture and are not at all reliable.

The basic difference between open-cell foam mats and closed-cell foam mats is that the closed-cell foam has sealed-cell chambers, while the open-cell type does not.

Open cells can soak up water, like a sponge. This is a great pity for the open cells make this type of foam bed very comfortable, although bulky. Closed cell is the nearest thing we have to the best available ground insulation. Because the cells are sealed, water is not absorbed, so you have a good waterproof mattress. Also, as the air is trapped in the cells, you do not need a thick piece: they come in a variety of thicknesses. For size, bulk, and efficiency, closed-cell foam wins hands down, and although many backpackers like a full-length piece of mat for winter work, most campers make do with a hip-length piece. This cuts down the load a little bit, and more important, cuts down on bulk. I often put some spare clothing, waterproofs, parka or something below my legs and feet to provide insulation there.

Stoves

Time was when inexperienced backpackers contemplating an outdoor cooking session were inspired by a once-popular genre of outdoors art: the camp fire. To many it was the archetypal camp scene: group of hikers congregated around a roaring fire, pots boiling merrily, the resinous scent of pine wood filling the nostrils, the fire providing warmth, light, and a source of heat for the cooking and brewing. To many it will be a nostalgic memory, drumming up visions of youthful forays into the

Cooking equipment
(Left) The Coleman Peak 1 stove produces a lot of heat for its size. It burns additive-free petrol (white gas) or a special fuel produced by Colemans, which can also be used on other stoves that burn white gas.

(Above) The classic backpacker's stove, the Svea, is known throughout the world. Also a petrol (white gas) burner, it is self-cleaning and requires no pressurizing. The aluminium cover serves also as a pot.

(Opposite) The Optimus Triple Fuel 199 Ranger burns, as the name indicates, three fuels: petrol (white gas), paraffin (kerosene), and methylated spirits (denatured alcohol). It is a powerful burner. The little pump pressurizes the stove so that it can be easily lit. The aluminium cover serves as a pot.

countryside. To many, even the scent of wood-smoke on the wind is enough to transport us back on sentimental journeys of delight; but think on. Romantic as the camp fire may be, such are the limitations of fond memory that we conveniently forget about the charcoal-black pots, and mugs which tainted everything within touching distance. We forget about the damp cold days when every source of fuel is wet and useless. We forget about the blackened faces, and the blackened hands, and the blackened clothes and the blackened sleeping bags, and we conveniently forget that the food was invariably foul.

Modern lightweight camping stoves may lack the romance of a campfire, they may seem cold and clinical and singularly lacking in aesthetic appeal. But they are functional. They are invariably

dependable. They are easily transportable, and most important of all, they offer a heat source in even the most inhospitable conditions in the world. Ethically too, in an outdoor world which is beginning to show signs of neglect and over-use, a stove allows us to keep ecosystem damage to a minimum. And that is perhaps the most important advantage of all.

TYPES OF STOVE
Conveniently, we can break down stove types to correspond with the fuels that are used to fire them.

Butane
Let us sort out some terminology. With increasing overlaps being made between European and American products, some of the nomenclature is becoming confusing. In Europe, for example, the

word "gas" or "gaz" means "vapour", not the gasoline of North America which is what Europeans call benzine or petrol. Similarly, the "white gas" referred to by many American stove manufacturers is a lead-free petrol, and nothing to do with gas vapour.

Butane stoves come in two parts: a fuel cartridge or canister, and the stove mechanism itself, consisting generally of a control valve and pot supports. The vast majority of butane stoves are vapour-feed, that is the butane fuel vapourizes in the cartridge, and the ensuing vapour is released into the stove and into the burner where it can be lit under control. The best known examples are the Camping Gaz Bluet and Globetrotter, made in France, and distributed worldwide. Another type of butane stove on the market, and one which I am convinced is destined to become more popular in the future is the liquid-feed stove. The fuel enters the stove as a liquid, usually by way of a wick built into the cartridge, and is vapourized there. What is the advantage? To realise the answer to that question, let us delve into the performance of butane gas in cold-weather conditions.

Butane fuel is a true gas, or vapour, liquified by compression and stored under extreme pressure in a sealed cartridge. If it were not stored under pressure, it would boil off, or vapourize, immediately. That is what happens when you open the control valve on the stove; the liquid butane vapourizes and is released into the burner of the stove, where it can be lit. Now, the pressure of the vapourized butane depends very much on temperature. The warmer it is, the higher the pressure of the vapour. At freezing point, its pressure would be fairly low, about the same as the pressure of the air around the stove if you are at sea level or close to it. In such a situation, the vapour will stay put in the

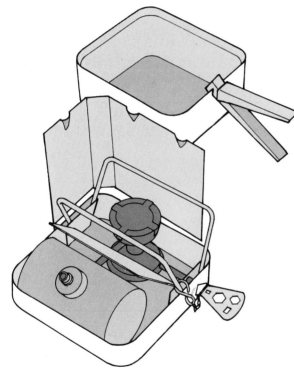

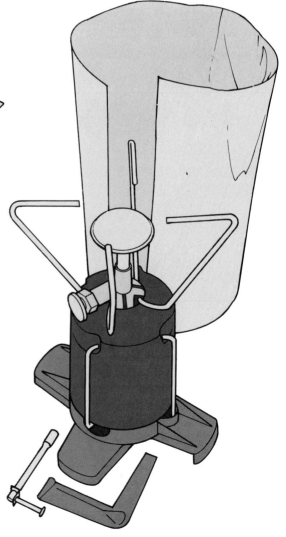

Cooking equipment (Left) The Optimus 8R is a popular backpacking stove. It is a petrol/gasoline burner that is self-cleaning as long as you use additive-free petrol (white gas). If you use an ordinary petrol, then you must clean the stove regularly.

(Right) The Bleuet S.200 is a butane stove that is clean, practical, and functions well. It is, however, a bit unstable, even with the supporting foot that is supplied with it.

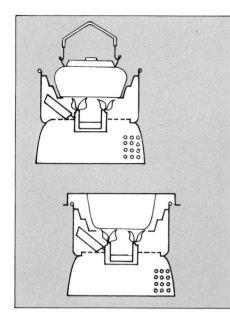

The Trangia methylated spirits (denatured alcohol) stove. The cutaway shows the kettle on the burner. The holes in the side of the burner are facing into the prevailing wind and provide baffled ventilation to the burner. To change the burning rate, the whole stove is turned so that the holes come more and more out of the wind, providing a not very exact simmer control. The lower illustration shows an alternative method of cooking, with the inverted frypan covering one of the stewpans, to provide a more intense heat.

(Right) The Trangia cook set packs down into a neat unit. It has several stew pans, a kettle, a pot grab, a frypan, and a pan lid.

cartridge. At even lower temperatures, the butane pressure drops even further. By this time it not only refuses to come out of the cartridge, but it may well even suck air in. Try it for yourself. Leave a butane stove in a freezer overnight, take it out in the morning and open the valve. There will be a momentary hiss as air is drawn into the cartridge. Then there will be nothing, at least not until the cartridge warms up to room temperature.

I wrote a magazine feature a few years ago on this aspect of butane stoves, and I suggested that butane was not for the serious backpacker. All right for picnics, or for use in warm sunny lowland weather, but certainly not for winter use. I was rather taken aback by the response I had from several loyal butane users, but the one which interested me most was a testimonial from a mountaineering expedition, who claimed that their butane stoves worked well in cold conditions at over 20,000 ft (6,000 m). I was surprised by this, and I must admit that I even doubted their integrity, but I know now how this apparent phenomenon takes place. At higher elevations, the pressure of the air around the stove is much lower than it is at sea level. At 10,000 ft (3,000 m) for example, the normal air pressure is about 12.3 p/s/i (3.1 k/s/cm), so a freezing-point cartridge will still release butane vapour and will start easily. At 20,000 ft (6,000 m), trouble with vapour release does not start until the temperature is around 0°F (−18°C); and that is cold indeed.

But back to the advantages of the liquid feed stove. Although vapour-feed butane stoves may work satisfactorily at high altitudes, they can present problems at lower altitudes in cold conditions. Liquid-feed stoves have better cold-weather starting characteristics. Because fuel is drawn out, or virtually poured out, low temperatures do not block fuel flow. Additionally, liquid-feed stoves are less temperature-dependent than vapour-feed stoves because conversion to vapour occurs in the stove body itself, which is quickly warmed by heat from the burner.

Generally speaking, butane stoves have many plus points over other types, especially for

A A new stove, recently developed by Primus, has an automatic lighting system that is excellent for lighting in windy conditions. The small fuel tank holds butane or propane for thirty minutes' use.

B The MSR Multi-fuel stove is excellent for melting snow, as it has a high output, despite its size. Some think that the tubing between the fuel bottle and the stove is a bit unwieldy and unstable.

C A cook set that comprises, from top to bottom, a lid that serves as a frypan, two medium-size pots, a windscreen, a Svea stove, and a stove base. Total weight 2 ¼ lb (about 1 kg).

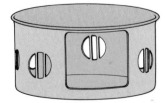

beginners and occasional campers. Simmer control is good, they are quick and simple to start, there is no fuel handling involved, and the stoves themselves are initially low cost when compared to others.

Obviously, the low performance in cold weather is a big minus for the vapour-feed butane stoves. The problem can be overcome to a certain degree by physically warming up the cartridge with body heat by cupping your hands around it, or by warming it up in the sleeping bag before you actually light it. It is a bit of a nuisance, but it does help. If you camp only in mid-summer, then there is no problem.

Fuel Comparisons

Advantages	Disadvantages

PETROL (Gasoline)

Advantages	Disadvantages
☐ Spilled fuel evaporates readily	☐ Priming required
☐ Stove fuel used for priming	☐ Spilled fuel highly flammable
☐ Fuel usually readily available	☐ Self-pressurizing stoves must be insulated from cold ground
☐ High heat output	

PARAFFIN (Kerosene)

Advantages	Disadvantages
☐ Spilled fuel does not easily ignite	☐ Priming required
☐ Stove can sit directly on the snow	☐ Spilled fuel does not evaporate easily
☐ Fuel usually readily available	
☐ High heat output	

BUTANE

Advantages	Disadvantages
☐ No fuel to spill	☐ High running costs
☐ No priming required	☐ Cartridge disposal is a problem
☐ Immediate maximum heat output	☐ Fuel must be kept above freezing for effective operation
	☐ Cannot change Gaz cartridges until empty
	☐ Low heat output

METHYLATED SPIRITS (Denatured alcohol)

Advantages	Disadvantages
☐ No priming required	☐ Higher fuel costs
☐ Immediate maximum heat output	☐ Fuel is heavy to carry
☐ Simple to operate	☐ Fuel burns quickly
☐ Spilled fuel evaporates readily	☐ Low heat output

Camping Gaz cartridges are totally sealed until they are actually pierced by the stove on installation. But an "empty" cartridge may well be merely low on fuel, or even worse, may not be functioning because of the low temperature problem. Take an inexperienced camper with a cartridge which appears to be empty, watch him remove a cartridge in a cloud of explosive butane, and there had better not be another stove, a candle or cigarette nearby. Make sure you read the directions with the stove, and make sure when you change a cartridge you do it as far away as possible from other heat sources.

Resealable cartridges are not without problems either. Very occasionally you will get one which does not reseal when you take it off the stove, and it spews butane all over the place. If that happens, screw it back onto the stove as quickly as possible and leave it there until it is finished. These points should, I hope, dispel any notion that gas stoves are "safer" than petrol stoves. Gas stoves are not foolproof. They were never designed for fools to use.

Propane stoves have been popular with family campers for years, but it is only recently that propane has come within the sphere of a backpacker. Some manufacturers are now producing resealable cartridges of propane/butane mix, and first impressions are that this could well be the answer to cold-weather performance problems. Propane vapourizes right down to below −50°F (−45.6°C) but must be kept under a pressure of about 124 p/s/i (31.5 k/s/cm) and thus must be contained in a fairly heavy steel cylinder, more or less excluding it from backpacking usage. The mix as used by some of the manufacturers still vapourizes much better than pure butane, does require heavy steel containers, and looks very promising indeed.

Priming

This is the phase of petrol/gasoline stove usage that is most dangerous. You must warm up the vaporizing tube before you actually light the stove. A small amount of fuel is poured into the shallow bowl at the end of the vaporizing tube and ignited. Much better is to use some burning paste, as in the picture. By the time the paste stops burning, the tube is warm, the fuel vaporizes, and the stove can be lit without a flare-up, which is what happens if non-vaporized fuel reaches the burner. *Be careful when priming!* Use burning paste rather than fuel when priming, but if you must use fuel, use only the minimum (don't overfill the priming bowl) and don't rush the priming process. Once the fuel has vaporized, it passes through the control valve to the burner itself. Most petrol/gasoline stoves have plate burners, which soon begin to glow red.

Petrol (gasoline) stoves

Gas stoves and petrol stoves are, in many ways, similar. Both fuels must be vapourized to burn efficiently. Petrol is wicked or, in some cases, forced by pressure into a vapourizing tube where heat from the burner converts it into vapour. It is then metered to the burner, mixed with air, and burned. The tank, vapourizing tube, and the burner are the three essential features.

Petrol-stove heat varies a little, but it is usually on the side of medium to high. Highest heat output belongs to the pump-pressurized fuel tanks, which makes them independent of external temperatures. Priming a pump stove can be a tricky business and takes a bit of practice. Most backpackers pressurize the stove, then briefly open the control valve to allow a small amount of fuel to run down the vapourizing tube into the priming cup. But it is so easy to release too much priming fuel, and this results in unwanted blazes.

A word about fuel. Ideally, we should use additive-free petrol, often referred to as white gas. This is not easy to find if you are backpacking in Europe, although Coleman Fuel, which is similar, is available in most backpacking shops. Most backpackers in Europe use 2-star petrol and find it quite adequate, although the lead in the petrol does tend to clog up sensitive systems rather quickly.

Possibly the most popular of all the white-gas stoves is the Svea 123 from Optimus, and it has earned a just reputation as a reliable little workhorse of a stove. If it has any faults it is possibly a little tippy, but that should not be a great problem if care is taken. The Svea is self-pressurizing and has an integral cleaning needle which is a distinct asset. The Optimus 8R and the Optimus 99 are also justly popular and are quickly gaining classic status. Basically, they are Sveas with the components shuffled around and arranged to fit into small square tin boxes. The performance of these three stoves is similar and could safely be put into the medium-output range. They all burn with a satisfying roar and once they are in full fling, the output is little affected by external temperatures. A word of warning though. In cold weather it is a good idea to insulate the bottom of the stove from the ground with a small pad of closed-cell foam, otherwise the output will steadily decline.

The Coleman Peak 1 stove is quickly gaining a good reputation, especially among winter backpackers, as a high-output stove. The Peak 1 is compact, fairly lightweight, 2 lb (0.9 kg), and has an integral windscreen, pot support, built-in cleaner, and a large burner.

The most expensive of all the stoves, and the beefiest burner, is the MSR GK from Mountain Safety Research in the United States. The MSR will burn white gas, petrol, paraffin, diesel fuel, aviation fuel, and it is claimed, peanut oil. It also burns like Krakatoa and is perfect for melting pot loads of snow and ice into water. Unfortunately, it does not simmer well, and there is a six-second delay between turning the valve and the flame being affected. That does not help the cordon-bleu chef... The MSR is another workhorse in the high-output category and is ideal for winter work. Minus points include the fact that should the stove go out, you have to remove the pot to re-light it. As I have said, it does not simmer, and although it has an integral sparker to light it initially, you still have to use a match to re-light the stove as the sparker will light petrol (or paraffin, or peanut oil) only in the priming bowl, not at the burner.

Paraffin (kerosene)
Paraffin stoves work similarly to petrol (gasoline) stoves but are far less volatile and are cheaper to operate. Paraffin is an excellent alternative to petrol, although it is a bit messier to work with. It feels oily and is slow to evaporate when spilled. It also smells strongly. On the plus side, it is very easily obtainable throughout the world, in varying grades admittedly, and it is very economical to run.

An example of the paraffin stove is the ever popular Optimus 00.

Methylated spirits (denatured alcohol)
One of the most popular stoves on the market is the Trangia meths stove. I would have little hesitation in recommending this stove for Boy Scouts, youth groups, beginners, and for family backpacking trips, as it is extremely safe and simple to use, and is probably the most stable of all the stoves we have looked at. Methylated spirits requires no priming, no pressurizing, and is simplicity itself to use. Both the Trangia and the Optimus Trapper models are designed so that their performance increases in windy weather, and both work extremely well in unsheltered outdoor situations. Unfortunately, meths is heavy and expensive, and neither the Trangia or the Trapper has good simmer control.

Windshields
Draughts and winds blowing around the tent make the use of a windshield round your stove virtually essential. Even when you cook in the bell end of the tent, there is always a slight draught blowing between the two skins of the tent. Quite often, a well-placed boot is enough to deter a minor draught from affecting the flame, but proper windshields are light, functional, and do not take up too much pack space. A large piece of aluminium foil, held up by some spare tent pegs, does an admirable job. A word of warning, though: when you improvise a windshield, make absolutely certain that there is sufficient ventilation round the fuel tank. Tanks on self-pressurizing stoves need to be warm to work but should *never* be allowed to become too hot to touch.

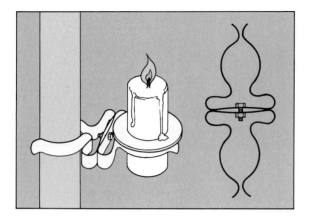

(Left) If you have an upright pole in your tent, you can make a candle-holder from two tool-clips. Don't mount the candle high and near the tent fabric. *Be careful* when you have a lighted candle in the tent. A safer alternative to the naked candle is a small lantern in which you place a short candle or night-light. The flame is protected at all times by the lantern's case.

(Centre) A battery-powered head lamp.

(Below and opposite) A couple of candles provide enough light for reading, especially if you rig up a windshield-cum-reflector from some aluminium foil. Protect the candles from upsets by putting them inside a small mug or pot.

Lighting

Despite the advances in camping equipment over the past few years, it seems strange that the most reliable, cheapest, lightest and most compact form of tent lighting is the humble candle. And it is in basically the same form as our ancestors have used for hundreds of years. My own recent tests show that a squat, 4 × 2½ in (10 × 6 cm) stearine candle will burn in still conditions for up to twenty hours. Knock off a couple of hours for the draughty conditions likely to be found in the average tent. That gives warmth and light for a ridiculously low hourly rate.

At first glance, the weight of such a candle, about ½ lb (¼ kg) may seem heavy, but the great advantage is that the candle can be cut to the size required for the duration of the trip. An ordinary weekend, with two tent nights, in winter would need half a candle. A candle this size is so compact that it takes little space and can be carried quite happily inside your mug. Alongside my candle, I also carry a small square of aluminium foil. Placed behind the flame, it will reflect a fair amount of heat and light, certainly enough for comfortable reading. Placed inside a small pot it is safe from upsets, and if positioned well in the bell end of the tent will also give adequate light for cooking.

Obviously, the main disadvantage of a candle is the fact that there is an open flame, and when *Homo sapiens* and open flames meet there is risk of fire. Another disadvantage is that candle light tends to flicker a bit when there is a draught, which is nearly always in a tent. This can be overcome to a great degree by sheltering the flame as much as possible with some form of windshield, even a well-placed boot.

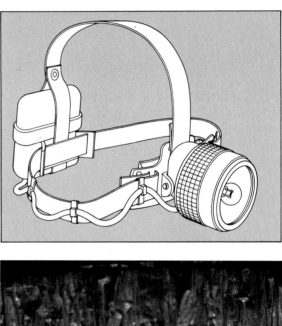

GAS

If you do not like the idea of a naked flame flickering inside the tent you may be willing to consider the extra weight of a gas lantern. Although heavier and bulkier than candles, gas lanterns burn with a satisfying hiss and steady light, and they also generate a fair amount of heat.

FLASHLIGHTS

The cost of batteries makes flashlights the most expensive form of tent illumination, but I think it is safe to say that a flashlight is an indispensable item of equipment, and not only for backpacking trips. Day walkers should also carry a flashlight as part of their emergency equipment. The very portability of a flashlight makes it indispensable; imagine going out into the dark on nature calls trying to carry a candle or gas lantern...

In summer a small flashlight is all that is necessary. Keep it in a safe place in the tent, quickly at hand for any nocturnal emergency that may occur. Carry spare batteries and a spare bulb.

In winter it tends to be a different story, and a much more substantial light is needed. My

flashlight's duties in winter range from pitching the tent in the dark, right through to checking for leaks or too much condensation in the wee small hours. What is needed is something that will give a good beam and will last for a reasonably long time; and at the same time be lightweight and compact. A headlamp provides the answer. The bulb and lens are fitted to an elasticized strap round your head, and a long wire connects it to a battery box which is carried in your pocket. Some newer headlamps have the batteries on the head strap too, eliminating the awkward necessity of long wires.

What we must bear in mind about using flashlights in winter is that low temperatures have an adverse effect on batteries, weakening them considerably until they can be warmed. My flashlight batteries are my constant bedmates in winter, as only the warmth from my body will keep it fully charged ready to produce a strong steady light when required. Also, bear in mind that as soon as the flashlight is switched on, the power from the battery starts to diminish, so use it only when you must, making do with a candle or gas lantern for long durations of light.

Cooksets

There is no reason at all why beginners should not set out initially with pots and pans pinched from their home kitchens. However, cooksets made specifically for lightweight camping have many advantages, not the least being that they tend to be far lighter in weight than domestic pots and pans. Look for strong bails or handles on the pots, tight-fitting lids, no internal ridges in the pots which will hold particles of food and make cleaning difficult, and pots which will conveniently nest inside each other.

Your choice will depend largely on how many people you will be catering for: a solo backpacker needs little more than one pot and a plastic mug, while a group of three or four may need a nesting set of three or four pots.

Most pots have bails for handles, but a very useful addition to your cookset is a pot grab, an aluminium pot holder. This saves much cursing from burnt fingers. Possibly the best is a spring-loaded steel model that gives a strong hold on loaded pots.

Drinking mugs

Most backpackers I know have a preference for a plastic mug of 1-pint (about ½ litre) capacity.

A collapsible water-bag with a spout in the bottom corner is a useful thing to have in camp, especially if you can hang it from a branch.

A "Le Grand Tetras" water bottles are of anodized aluminium, do not taint, and are extremely strong. They come in a variety of shapes and sizes.

B Some different types of nesting pots and pans. Only take with you what you reckon on using.

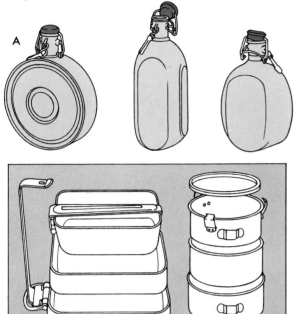

C The Sierra Cup, popular among many backpackers.

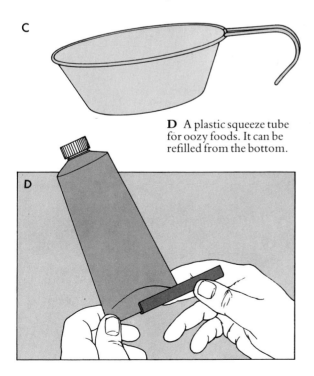

D A plastic squeeze tube for oozy foods. It can be refilled from the bottom.

Others, though, prefer the additional weight of enamel mugs. Stainless steel mugs tend to get hot and burn the lips, although in the United States, and increasingly in Europe, backpackers are using a squat stainless-steel drinking cup universally known as the Sierra Cup. This cup has a curved wire bale so that it can be hung under your belt. Strangely enough, it really is not a very practical vessel. Its wide rim cools down food and drink very quickly, it is heavy for its size, it is not big enough for a decent drink, and its narrow bottom lacks stability; and yet, thousands upon thousands are sold every year. The Sierra Cup is in fact, more of a badge of office than a drinking vessel, the sign that you are indeed a backpacker. I have found the Sierra Cup quite handy for scooping water out of rivers to fill water containers, or for adding cold water to the pot on the stove. It is also good for drinking whisky from, as it does not taint as a plastic mug would. Ideally, a drinking mug should have at least ½-litre (1 pint) capacity, the working size of most soup and stew mixes. Mark the inside of it at the half-full mark, so you can carefully gauge amounts of water for cooking.

Eating utensils

Plates are not necessary. Eat straight from the pot. The food stays warmer longer, and you have less washing up to do at the end of the day, an important point if water is scarce. The same goes for forks; you do not need them. A plastic spoon, or a steel dessert spoon is quite sufficient for mixing food, stirring, measuring and carrying the stuff to your mouth. An extra luxury is a small teaspoon for putting sugar into tea or coffee.

Backpackers tend to adopt a strange affinity for their knives, perhaps as a throwback to days when knives were indeed important as eating tools, skinning tools, and even weapons. The gadgeteering Swiss Army Knife, with a thousand and one different blades, is at first glance the ideal tool for backpacking; but think again. How often will you need a tool which takes stones out of horses' hooves, or a corkscrew, or a toothpick? Really, all we require is something to spread butter or jam onto a biscuit, or cut some cheese or meat. There is a lighter and less complicated Swiss Army Knife available, with only two or three blades, plus a can and bottle opener. If you are taking canned food with you, don't forget a can opener. You can buy a small can opener and tie it to a length of brightly coloured cord, so that it can be found easily.

Food and water containers

Mountain-equipment stores carry a good range of plastic food-containers, bags, and bottles. The plastic bag is a godsend to backpackers, and every backpacker should become a plastic-bag collector. These are good for wrapping food, individually wrapping meals, and the larger ones can be used for waterproofing stuff sacks containing clothes or sleeping-bag.

Plastic boxes are handy for storing and carrying biscuits, crackers, cheese, or any crushable food, while small plastic pill-boxes are ideal for sugar, salt, pepper, and spices. Camera-film canisters make ideal salt and pepper holders. Plastic squeeze tubes are first-class for holding jam, honey, peanut butter, margarine, and any other oozy food. The tube has a clip bottom to allow you to refill when necessary.

Plastic water-bottles should have a fairly wide mouth for easy filling and should be large enough to hold enough water for cooking at least one meal. Better are the nylon-covered plastic bags which have a little rubber spout in the corner. These waterbags hold a couple of gallons and are extremely convenient for camp use. There is nothing more annoying than having to run back and forth to the stream every time you want a drink or want to start cooking.

Chap. 6

CAMPING TECHNIQUES

Campcraft

All day long we've been wandering along, enjoying the fresh air and the freedom, but now our limbs are beginning to feel rather heavy, and we have a gnawing sensation in the gut which suggests that we have had enough of peanuts and chocolate and that it is high time we had a proper slap-up meal. The search for a camp site begins.

CHOOSING A CAMPSITE
Take your time in looking for the place to camp. Start searching in mid afternoon, and if you find an ideal spot, stick with it. If you leave this task until last thing, when you are really tired and hungry, you will end up grabbing the first piece of dry ground you come across, with little thought for how flat the pitch is and what direction the wind is coming from. Camp sites are important, not only from the comfort and safety point of view, but because a large number of the memories you will relish in years to come will be of perfect pitches: lying outside the tent watching the sun sink in an explosion of colour; the pitch by the waterfall which sang you to sleep; the beautiful camp site by the river, where the cows came in the morning to drink, their bells clanging as they sauntered off to be milked.

A good view from the tent door is a must for me, but equally important is a flat level spot, not in a hollow, with shelter on the side of the prevailing wind. Ideally, water should not be too far away either. Your spot should be well drained, and the ground should be firm enough to hold your tent pegs firmly.

A level camp site is important. Try sleeping with your head downhill and you will wake up in the morning with one almighty headache. Pitch on a side slope and you will spend the night subcon-sciously wrestling with yourself, fighting against the slope. Remember too, that nylon sleeping-bag covers tend to slip around a bit, so if you are on any slope at all, you will spend the night bracing against gravity. A flat pitch is a must.

All right, so modern tents are strong and windproof and if you wanted to prove that point you could pitch on the most exposed site possible and spend the night listening to the wind buffeting you and wondering, with a tinge of doubt, whether your tent is really that weatherproof. Avoid the worry and choose a pitch with some shelter: rocks, stone wall, a hedge, or a copse of trees (although the noise of the wind surf in the tree tops will probably keep you awake all night). Bear in mind too, that winds occasionally veer during the night. If available shelter is inadequate, then pitch your tent tail into the wind, presenting the gusts with the best wind foil you can. Never pitch with the door of the tent facing the wind direction. Even a very slight breeze will play havoc with your cooking stove and candle.

Water sources
Availability of water is, of course, a prime consideration when choosing a camp site. In mountain areas, there is invariably a stream or river close by, but in rural farm areas, for example, fresh water may be at a premium and the backpacker may have to ask at farms.

Always treat natural water supplies with suspicion; quite often they will be polluted. Mountain-top water tends to be good, but always check a little upstream to make sure there is not a dead sheep or a dead deer lying in the water course. Purifying tablets help, but make the water taste foul. Water purifiers are also available, but I do not know very many backpackers who actually use them. They seem a bit gimmicky to me.

(Above) Wind shelter is always a good idea. Pitch on the lee side of a wall or some big rocks.

(Right) By pitching your tent just under the brow of a hill the worst of the wind will be avoided.

Choosing a campsite
Finding a suitable pitch is the first step toward an enjoyable night. Look for a spot away from the trail and away from other camps. The site should be level and the ground fit for lying on. Clear the site of small stones and anything else likely to disturb your sleep. Some backpackers lie down on the ground to test it first.

If you have left it too late to search out a pitch for your tent that is windsheltered, or if any other circumstances make it necessary for you to set up camp in a spot that is exposed to the wind, you will simply have to make the best of it. Pitch your tent with its tail into the wind. Hopefully, the wind will not veer during the course of the night. Drive your pegs as deep as possible into the ground in order to anchor the guys securely. If possible, reinforce the pegs with rocks.

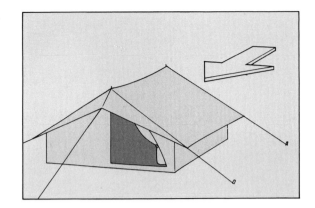

When looking for a campsite, try to find the most beautiful spot you can. Think about where the sun will rise and whether it will warm your tent—you may need its warmth to dry out. I like to have a view from my porch. That is what I want to remember about the site.

(Opposite) Lakeside campsites are always tempting but are invariably cold places to camp. Cool air drops and warm air rises, and that cool air must have somewhere to drop to—right down the hillside to the lake. Choose a ledge higher up the slope, and the cool air will roll past you. Remember if you are thinking of lakeside camping in summer that the mosquitos thrive there and will welcome your arrival.

(Right) Collect your drinking and cooking water upstream, wash your dishes downstream. Your latrine should be well away from the camp, any water source, and nowhere near a spot that might be chosen in the future by some other camper for his campsite. Bury your waste, burn toilet paper and bury it, and cover it all well.

126

CHOOSING A WINTER CAMPSITE

A badly chosen pitch in summer need not be disastrous. More often than not lack of suitable shelter may only result in an annoyingly uncomfortable night. In winter, it is a different story.

The main consideration in winter is the availability of water. Melting snow or ice for drinking water can be a long and tedious process which uses up a great deal of precious fuel. The second consideration is that there are no dangers about. By this I mean that you should not pitch on an avalanche slope, under snow falling from trees, exposed to excessive wind, or in areas which attract drifting snow.

We have discussed avalanches in another chapter, but remember to stay well clear of any pitch at the direct foot of a slope, out of narrow gullies or on steep treeless terrain; these make natural avalanche paths. All the snow which falls on mountain slopes will either melt or, sooner or later, come sliding down to settle in a more stable position. Make certain that your little tent is not down there should that happen.

Avoid camping under trees. Many folk are mistaken in thinking that a few trees are just the thing for a bit of shelter but they forget that snow, especially soft, wet, heavy snow, often falls from the tree tops, and if your tent is directly underneath, the chances are that it will be flattened. Stay in the lee of trees, but not directly underneath, and beyond the drift line such lees create. The other danger from trees is that a strong wind may well tear off branches, or even worse, blow a tree down.

PITCHING ON SNOW

Once you have selected your pitch, someone should set about the routine task of fetching water and putting on a brew. While that is being done, someone else should begin to flatten out the area where the tent is to be pitched. This stamped-out platform should be slightly larger than the tent itself, and the more you stamp on it the more compact and firm the surface will become. Check that it is even and flat, for the surface will soon freeze, and any lumps and bumps will feel like concrete under your body when you settle in for the night.

PEGGING THE TENT

There are several methods of staking out a tent, depending on the weather conditions prevailing at the time. If it is dead calm, it may remain so for the night, but you cannot depend on it. So, pitch your tent tightly, then if the weather does get worse, you will have been prepared for it. Long angled pegs, sunk into the snow at a hard angle will probably suffice, but if you suspect that it will be windy, you will have to use an extra, or alternative method. Ice axes, sunk well into the snow, make secure anchors for the main load-bearing guys.

SUB-ZERO NIGHTS

Damp boots will rapidly freeze if left outside, or even if they are left in the bell end of the tent. Putting on frozen boots is one of the most miserable things imaginable, and it takes a good few miles of walking before they begin to thaw out. If the weather is very cold, take them to bed with you, or at least use them as a pillow. Place them on their sides, toes pointing out, and put your clothes over them. You now have a fairly comfortable pillow, and the boots are well protected from the cold.

Another bedmate you may have to consider in winter is a plastic or aluminium water bottle. Water freezes very quickly if left outside during sub-zero temperatures, so fill the bottle with enough water to see you through breakfast and either take it to bed with you, or wrap it up in some spare clothing and place it between you and your friend, or in the crook of your knees.

WINTER CAMPING PROBLEMS

Dampness can spoil even a mid-summer camping trip. Wet conditions day in and day out can make life intolerable. The first thing to do is avoid bringing any wetness in the form of rain or snow inside the tent with you, either from your clothes or boots. Take off your raingear before you enter the tent. The same goes for boots. Brush off any snow that has fallen on your clothes. If any dampness does get inside the tent, mop it up with a small sponge or cloth.

Spindrift is a very fine, dry snow which blows about in the wind, almost like dust. It is a part of snow camping which can drive you virtually insane. In very cold conditions, this fine snow finds its way into every little crack and niche, and can even penetrate the fine insect netting on tent doors. If there is a millimetre of space where the tent-door zips meet, then you can bet your bottom dollar that spindrift will come pouring in there. In this type of weather conditions, the only thing you can do is lie in wait for spindrift, and brush it out just as soon as it comes in before it gets a chance to melt. Spindrift like this is normally a high-altitude problem, but it occasionally occurs in lower levels too.

When backpacking in winter, rest stops are important. On a fine day with little wind, you can set up a wind shelter by sticking tent poles or walking staffs into a bivouac sack (storm shell) and standing them in the snow. Then dig a place for your feet, spread out an insulation mat to sit on, and have something to eat and drink.

(Inset) If the wind is so strong that you cannot set up a bivouac sack as described, you can crawl into the sack after digging a place for your feet. Take in your packs with you.

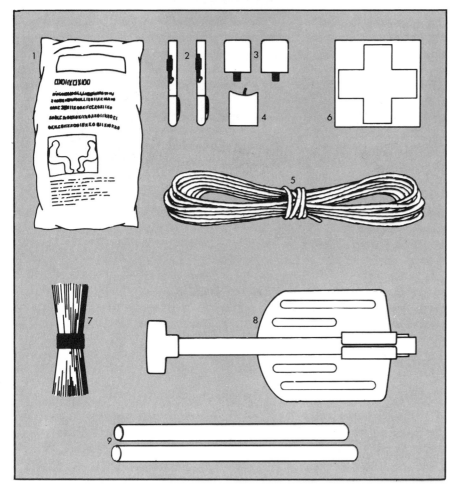

Winter equipment
(1) A roomy bivouac sack, at least 2 m (6 ft) long, for two to three people. *(2)* A "rocket pen" for shooting up emergency flares *(3)*. *(4)* Stearine candles to give light and warmth in a snow shelter. *(5)* A safety line of red nylon, about 20 m (66 ft) long and 4 mm (1/6 in). *(6)* First-aid kit. *(7)* Snow brush for clothes, boots, and pack, to keep the tent interior dry. *(8)* Small collapsible snow shovel of aluminium. *(9)* PVC plastic tubing for temporary repairs to tent poles.

Tent living

Camp life is surprisingly simple. In good summer weather, when we walk on until dusk, the tent is merely a sleeping place, offering some protection in the event of rain or biting insects. There are no problems about drying clothes, drying boots, or even drying tents. In fact, there are often situations in high summer where you will not even have to unpack the tent at all; just lay out your sleeping-bag, crawl into it, and nod off.

Normally though, life is not quite as simple. On extended trips there are chores to be done; boots to be proofed or waxed, socks and shirts to be washed and dried, perhaps there are some minor repairs to be carried out to clothes or camping kit. Even on short trips, you may find yourself having to dry off socks, shirts or even tents before you can set off in the morning.

PITCHING CAMP
On discovering a suitable camp site, the first thing to be done is to get the stove going. That means by the time you have pitched the tent, you will have a warm cup of tea or coffee waiting for you. If you have companions with you, delegate someone to this chore, while the rest pitch the tents. In bad weather, it is psychologically beneficial to pitch the waterproof flysheet, and then, before hanging up the inner tent inside, get under the fly, strip off your waterproofs, which may be dripping wet, put them inside a polybag or stuff sack so that they do not get everything else wet, and enjoy your brew-up in dry comfort. It is vital, at any time of the year, to keep the inner tent as dry and comfortable as possible, so it is silly to try and hang it up to the flysheet when you are wearing dripping wet clothes. It is also sociable to get under the flysheet and enjoy that first camp brew-up together.

Once you have relaxed for a bit, you can proceed to hang up the inner tent in dry comfort. Then, drag your pack into the bell end of the flysheet, and unpack all the necessities: sleeping-bag, insulation mat, stove, food, flashlight, and book.

Camp cooking
If you cook in the bell end of the tent, everything is confined to a small space and will not easily get lost. If it is a bit chilly, you can even get into your sleeping-bag and do your cooking and eating from there.

130

Luxury in camp: cool your first-night-out wine in a bubbling brook…

… and do your cooking from the comfort of a hammock.

In dry weather, I like to haul my sleeping-bag from its stuff sack and fluff it up by holding it with both hands at the neck and giving it a good shake. This allows the down or synthetic filling to decompress, and fill with air. I then lay it down to air, over the tent, or perhaps over some nearby rocks, for a while. Sleeping-bags can become a bit smelly after extended use, so it is a good idea to air them at every opportunity. If your sleeping-bag has a side zipper, open the bag out fully, and let as much air in and about it as possible.

With tent pitched, insulation pad laid out, and sleeping-bag stretched out to air, it is time to find a kitchen. In bad weather and in winter the bell end of my tent becomes a joint storage area and kitchen. My pack always lives in there, where it is easily accessible, and it is not allowed into the main living area of my tent. Packs tend to have buckles, frames, and zippers, which could possibly damage the groundsheet of the inner tent. The pack may also be dirty or wet, both good reasons for leaving it outside my main living area. Some backpackers like to leave the pack outside all night long, covered by a large plastic bag of the type used for garbage disposal. If you do not have a lot of space in the bell end of your tent, or if you do not have a bell end at all, then this is a good idea. You can even buy bona-fide waterproof pack covers which can be used to cover the pack when it is being carried in wet weather, or to protect the pack when it is left outside during the night.

CAMP COOKING

Cooking is one of the most important activities of backpacking life. After your day on the trail, you are going to have one whale of an appetite. Lightweight camping, you would perhaps imagine, dictates spartan meals: nuts and raisins, cold meats, cheese, with very little in the gourmet stakes. I have known backpackers live for a week on cold food and water. They save themselves the hassle of cooking; they do not have to carry the extra weight of a stove, and they have very little washing-up to do. Cold food and water can offer all the necessary fats and carbohydrates to keep on the move efficiently, and for those who eat to live, as opposed to "live to eat", then this may very well be an acceptable way of doing it. But it does not necessarily have to be so.

I am one of those folk whose mouth begins to water at the very thought of good, well-cooked food. I can rarely allow three or four hours to pass without the subject of food entering my thoughts, and one of the real highlights of my backpacking day is to cook (yes, I actually enjoy the cooking part of it, much to my wife's amazement) and enjoy a good meal.

Cooking in the bell end of a tent can be hazardous, unless some care is taken. Check that the stove is perfectly stable and sheltered from breezes. A sheet of aluminium foil makes a superb windshield. Support it with some spare tent pegs. Many backpackers encircle their stove completely with aluminium foil, but I do not subscribe to this. Heat, reflected from the foil, can cause a pressure stove or butane stove to overheat, and possibly explode. All that is necessary is some protection from the breeze, which should not be strong if you have pitched your tent correctly anyway.

With stove, water bag, and food all laid out in the bell end of the tent, I like to lie on my insulation mat and cook from a prone position. Or else I will sit cross-legged at the front of the tent. If I am sharing the tent with a friend, I have found it a good idea to delegate only one person to cook the complete meal. Otherwise, there will be too many hands fumbling about in what is a rather cramped area, and accidents could easily occur. Most backpacking duos, or trios, work out a system for cooking and washing up. One cooks breakfast, while the other looks after the dinner, and the one who cooks escapes the washing-up chores, although it makes life a lot simpler, and cleaner, to scour out pots and mugs as soon as you have used them.

If the weather is good, cook outside. Find a camp kitchen by some rocks, or ideally, on a large rocky slab by a tumbling stream. In group backpacking, this is the finest way to manage a kitchen. Everybody can now lend a hand, with plenty of space available. With two or three stoves all blasting away, it becomes possible to prepare feasts.

BREAKFAST

I wake early when I am out there on the trail. The best part of the day to be up and about is early morning, so I am usually anxious to get breakfast over so that I can get packed up and away. Having said this, breakfast is an important meal, the base of your fuel for the rest of the day, so it is important to get something inside you which will work away slowly and efficiently.

My first action on waking is to light the stove. I never bring it inside the actual tent, as I can think of nothing more horrendous than a burning tent while I am still cocooned in a sleeping-bag. The bell end of the tent is the place to light the stove and boil up

Some tips for cooking and eating: put your drinking mug or your gas stove inside a boot to avoid spills. Spare tent pegs can also be used to hold a tippy stove steady.

132

A hearty breakfast will start you off properly on your day's hiking, snacks on the trail keep your blood sugar at the right level, and a sound dinner is a good reward for the day's work, something to look forward to and to enjoy. A light supper at bedtime will help you relax and sleep well.

some water for the day's first cup of tea or coffee. In actual fact, I boil up a little more water than I need for my cup of tea, because I will be using some of it to pour over a pot of muesli or porridge. I personally prefer a hot breakfast, and the oats, nuts, and raisins that make up muesli suits me ideally. Pour some dried milk over the dry ingredients, add some hot water and some brown sugar, and you have a warming and appetising starter to the day. By using the one pot of water for the hot drink and the hot muesli, it means I can eat and drink together. Usually, I eat the hot muesli while the tea cools enough to drink, and then I drink it with some oatcakes or wheat crackers and cheese. Many folk dislike the idea of eating cheese for breakfast, but it is a good food with plenty of fat and protein in it. It is, in fact, an ideal food to start the day. It is a good idea to leave a little hot water in the pan once you have used up what you need for cooking. This means that you can use the remaining hot water for cleaning up the mug and pan. I use a sponge which has a coarse plastic scrubber on one side of it. A scrub round with the sponge pad, a rinse out with some cold water, and the pot and pan are ready to be packed away, with the cleaning sponge living inside the packed pot.

Other backpackers will prefer a real cooked breakfast and will be happy enough to spend a considerable time preparing it. My simple yet nourishing breakfast can be easily prepared from the comfortable confines of my sleeping-bag. I can then pack up all the cooking gear and the food, all the bits and pieces that live inside the tent with me, get dressed, pack my sleeping-bag, all without having to leave the shelter of the tent. I do not relish the idea of cooking fatty bacon and eggs and sausages from my sleeping-bag. Fried foods have the habit of sizzling and splashing fat all over the place, and the only place you can really cook a meal of this type is in the open air. For this reason I tend not to bother. Having said that, there is no finer scent to the air first thing in the morning than the smell of frying bacon.

If you do insist on a fried breakfast, you will need something to grease the pan. Oil is the ingredient which comes to mind, but oil is difficult to carry in small quantities and would have sorrowful results if it were spilt in the pack. Butter or margarine, carried in a refillable squeeze tube, can be used for frying and has the added advantage that it can also be used for spreading on bread or biscuits, or just for dolloping into soups, stews, or curries to give some added fatty body. There is nothing like a good hot, fatty soup in winter to stick to your ribs.

Pick your trail snack as you go along. Nature has a rich larder to provide you with that something extra for your menu. Wild onions and garlic will make any freeze-dried dish delicious. Mushrooms should be picked with care. Pick only those mushrooms that you are *certain* are not poisonous. The hiker in the picture is picking rose hips. The outer rind contains lots of vitamin C and can be eaten raw or cooked. Rose hip tastes best after the first frost. Wild strawberries, blackberries, blueberries, and other easy-to-identify fruits are a welcome addition to your morning muesli.

TRAIL SNACKS

With breakfast over, and everything packed away in the rucksack, I usually start eating lunch… Constant nibbling as you walk will fuel the body much more efficiently than eating nothing at all until lunch time and then filling the stomach with a large and heavy meal. As I walk, I carry in my pocket a plastic bag of GORP, which every true American backpacker knows stands for Good Old Raisins and Peanuts. I like to think of the word gorp as an onomatopoeia for the various bits and pieces of goodies which find their way into this snack bag of mine. Nuts and raisins most certainly form the basis of it, but I also add orange and lemon peel, some brown sugar, chocolate crumbs, coconut, and some granola or oat flakes. It is good chewy stuff, is full of protein, and often acts as a quick and efficient energy-booster in the event of my running prematurely out of steam. Quite often I will also carry some chocolate with me, and that makes a pleasant change, although it does tend to make one thirsty.

Although I munch away fairly steadily at my gorp and chocolate, there is a psychological benefit in actually stopping for an hour or so at lunch time, and putting on a brew of tea or coffee. Don't make a full-scale meal of it though, as you will feel bloated and tired afterwards, and totally unwilling to get up, put on your pack, and walk. If you enjoy coffee or tea at lunchtime, it is well worth while packing your stove, pots, lighter, and mug into the side pockets of your rucksack, so that you can get to them quickly and easily. I tend to keep my tea bags and sugar in a separate container to the rest of my food for this very purpose, and keep that container close beside the stove.

DINNER

Generally, come mid-afternoon, I begin to look forward to dinner and spend some miles dreaming of what I am going to eat, and just how I am going to cook it.

Once I have selected my pitch, I usually put a pan of water on the stove to boil. By the time the water is bubbling away, I will have the tent set up, my sleeping-bag fluffed up and laid inside it, and I will be just ready for a cup of coffee. In winter time, this quick ready brew can be a lifesaver. As you walk along in the course of a cold day your body generates enough heat to keep you fairly warm, but once you stop to pitch camp, you quickly cool down and by the time you strip off your outer clothes and get into the shelter of the tent, you may be frozen stiff. To have a hot cup of tea or coffee thrust into your frozen hands at that very moment is sheer heaven. Additionally, a body warmed by a hot drink will warm up a sleeping-bag a lot quicker than a shivering body.

In summer, I drink my cup of tea or coffee, and then wander off for a while to explore the vicinity of my campsite, and in winter, I usually enjoy my hot drink over a good book. Invariably, I take a short snooze, before waking up to cook dinner.

Dinner is the main meal of the day, and in some cases, the highlight of the day. Being a lover of food, I try and make a bit of an event out of dinner and often will spend a couple of hours cooking and eating several courses. I like to begin with soup, usually the one-cup variety. Boil up some water and, while that is heating, mix the contents of the soup packet with a stock cube, a few herbs, and a dollop of margarine or butter. Remember to boil up more water than you need, so that you will have some left over to clean out your pot or mug, or whatever you drink your soup from. I never carry plates or bowls with me, preferring to eat straight from the pot. My kit contains two pots and a frying-pan-cum-lid, and that combination is adequate for two people.

As I eat my soup from one pot, the other is back on the stove heating water for the main course. That may be a freeze-dried meal like turkey tetrazinni, shrimp creole, beef Madras curry, boeuf Bourguignonne, or some other exotic sounding dish, or it may be a dehydrated meal. The difference between freeze-dried and dehydrated is simple. Freeze-dried food can be cooked by simply pouring boiling water over the contents of the packet. You can then eat it more or less immediately. Dehydrated food takes a little bit longer, since it must be simmered for a while before you can eat it.

Quite often I will carry a small tin of minced meat or stew, and eat it with powdered potato which has been doctored with some margarine, some cheese, and maybe some bacon pellets. Or preferably, I will use some quick-cook Ramen noodles or rice. Ramen noodles only need some boiling water poured over them, a stir around and they are ready to eat, and you can flavour them with stock cubes, herbs and spices, or sauces. Once you have prepared

Always boil more water than you need for cooking. The excess can then be used to clean the pots and plates immediately after use.

the noodles or rice, put them on top of the pot that is on the stove. That way you will not only heat up what is in the pot, the mince, or stew, or curry, or whatever, but you will also keep the noodles or the rice warm as well, until you are ready to eat it all together.

Bear in mind that it is quite a hassle lighting and re-lighting a stove in the course of preparing several courses, so try and cook the complete meal without having to turn the stove off. This can be done easily by always having one course cooking, as you are eating the previous one. And always have some hot water handy for scouring out the pots between courses.

A sweet course is often enjoyable. Quick-cook custard, quick-cook semolina, and quick-cook rice are marvellous backpacking standbys. All these convenience foods require is some hot water and a mix. Add some powdered or condensed milk and sugar or honey to any of them for a sweet, sickly, delightful course which will have you crawling away from the stove for a rest from sheer gluttony. These sweets are also good with some jam or honey from a plastic squeeze-tube, or some cinnamon and apple flakes. Delicious.

Finish dinner with a brew. Tea bags and coffee bags are a backpacker's best friend. Several years ago, I weaned myself off milk, so I do not have the inconvenience of having to carry it now, but powdered milk nowadays seems to be very acceptable.

Alcohol is generally not a good idea when you are backpacking, but there is something totally luxurious about leaning back after a good meal with a whisky or a brandy and a large cigar.

CONTAINERS

The simple plastic bag has made an incredible difference to our lives. It is probably the ultimate in lightweight, watertight containers. Make sure that you can easily identify what you put in it, though. Label the bags, and tie off the top with simple quick twist ties. Dried foods are best put inside a double plastic bag. In that way, if one bag tears, the food is still protected, and you can never have too many bags around you anyway.

One up from the plastic bag is the small plastic box with a snap-on lid. You can buy these from most hardware or camping stores, in a variety of shapes and sizes. Ask your local pharmacist or drugstore for the little plastic bottles that are often used for pills and tablets, and are usually thrown out. Make sure you thoroughly clean them out before you use them, though.

I often use 35-mm-film containers for salt, pepper, and some mixed herbs and spices, with different coloured lids so that I know what is what.

Nutrition

When backpacking, the body must be thought of as an engine, a complex piece of machinery which must be properly fuelled for maximum efficiency. If not fuelled by the proper constituents, in the proper proportions, the engine will break down; and this seize-up could very well have serious consequences if it happens miles from help. Nutrition is the process by which food is broken down and used either to create energy or build body tissue. Energy is needed initially just to live. If a normal adult male stayed in bed all day he would still need about 1,000 calories just to keep his body functioning, his heart beating, and his temperature stable, without losing weight. It follows, therefore, that if it is very cold, the calorie intake must be increased because more energy is required simply to keep the body warm. If

you happen to be cross-country skiing or backpacking with a heavy load, your calorie intake may have to soar to 6,000 or more, so it is vitally important that attention is given to what you eat.

You must take in the correct balance of protein, carbohydrate, vitamins, and so on, so that the body can function efficiently. Too much of one thing or a lack of another can lead to problems.

It is important, therefore, to understand the special role each of these food constituents play in keeping us going.

PROTEINS

Proteins are needed for growth, build-up, and repair of muscle tissue. The average adult needs about 3 oz (85 g) of protein daily, of which half should be from animal origin. Major sources of protein are milk, fish, meat, and eggs. Vegetarians need a daily intake of about 5 oz (142 g) from other sources. Proteins are really molecules of amino acids, and all but eight of the amino acids can be synthesized by the body. These eight, the essential amino acids, have to be consumed regularly. The richest source of these proteins are animal products, which is why vegetarians need a bigger daily intake because the concentrations are not so high in vegetable matter. Meat, fish, cheese, eggs, and milk all contain all the "essential" amino acids, while most vegetables lack one or other of these "essentials".

Because children are still growing, their protein requirements for body building is much higher, and they should be consuming daily two to three times the adult intake.

Protein sources of animal origin
Cheese is the richest source, about one-third of its weight being protein. Lean bacon and lean beef are about 25% protein, eggs about 12%, and milk 3.5%.

Protein sources of vegetable origin
Broad beans and dried peas are about 20% protein, bread is about 6.5%, and potatoes are 2.2%.

FATS

Fats are important because they do provide some essential fat-soluble vitamins, but experts disagree over whether there is a minimum daily requirement. The body must have fatty acids, and one of the most important reasons for eating fat is that it makes us feel full. It is fat in the stomach that gives us the feeling that we have just eaten a big meal. We could quite easily take in our calorie requirement in protein food, but we would feel cheated if we did not experience the "full-up" feeling afterwards. If we take in too much fat, and do not work it off, it gets stored in the body.

If we are on a long trip, or taking part in endurance events, we can break down this body fat, but it is a very uneconomic use of energy. It takes about 10% more oxygen to release energy from fat than from carbohydrate, which means there is less oxygen left to pump through the muscles. There is also the much more important disadvantage that you have to carry that extra weight around with you. Butter and margarine are about 80% fat, cheese is about one third fat, and fatty meat is obviously another good source. Fat is only metabolized if the body has carbohydrates to get the reaction going, which is another indication of why it is so important to get the balance of food intake right.

Medical opinion has recently suggested we should reduce our intake of fat from animal sources and switch to polyunsaturated fats from vegetable matter. The argument has now become very clouded, however, with butter manufacturers producing as much evidence to illustrate how bad margarine is for you, as the margarine industry has against butter…

CARBOHYDRATES

These are the real energy givers. Starches and sugars in the food are broken down and stored mainly in the liver and muscles as polysaccharide glycogen. When the body needs energy, the glycogen is converted back to glucose, the "fuel" that is needed to drive and heat muscles. Unfortunately, if we take in too much carbohydrate, the surplus is simply converted to fat.

Flour can be up to 75% carbohydrate, potatoes 20%, bananas 20%, and carrots 10%. The advantage of carbohydrate as an energy giver is that it can be reconstituted without the need for oxygen. That is true until the normal source of glucose has been used up and the body has to draw on its fat reserves which does take oxygen.

The Sports Nutrition Division of Wander, the Swiss dietary food company, has looked at the problem of sugar loading. Often in the past, walkers, climbers, and backpackers would swallow handfuls of glucose tablets when they felt fatigued. Glucose is a simple sugar and is easily and quickly digested, but it can sometimes be counter-productive. Glucose taken in this way raises the blood-sugar content, which triggers increased insulin secretion. One of the functions of insulin is to control the amount of sugar in the blood, so too much can mean a quick reduction in the glucose level and a feeling of dizziness and weakness, known as hypoglycaemia. More often than not this can quickly be overcome, but it can be a very serious problem if you happen to be climbing at the time, or if bad weather strikes.

Although you do not get that instant "shot" that glucose gives you, the experts believe it is better that you try to absorb more complex carbohydrates which take longer to break down and give a more controlled blood-sugar release.

VITAMINS

The amount of vitamins we need to take in depends on the amount of activity to be pursued. For very physical pursuits it is vital to absorb as much of the Vitamin B range as possible, because this is the group of vitamins needed to convert carbohydrates into usable sugars. It also encourages stamina. Vitamin C is necessary because the body can neither produce it nor store it. We can get our supplies from fresh fruit and vegetables, of course. Lack of vitamin A leaves you vulnerable to infection, and Vitamin K is necessary for blood clotting.

The great problem with vitamins is our general lack of knowledge about them. We are slowly understanding how they work, and generally we can get our daily requirement from a well-balanced diet.

MINERALS

The body needs a number of basic minerals which it absorbs in the form of mineral salts—sodium, potassium, magnesium, phosphorus, calcium, chloride, iron, and iodine. Calcium is required for bones and teeth, and the best source is milk. Iron is needed for the synthesis of haemoglobin, and a deficiency leads to anaemia. Haemoglobin is vital for pushing oxygen round the body. Best sources are meat, eggs, spinach, and some other vegetables. A special group of minerals, the "electrolytes", which includes sodium, potassium, magnesium, calcium, and chloride, is lost through sweating, and it is essential that these minerals be replaced. If the body's reserves of minerals run short, the first signs are usually muscle cramps, and then severe muscle contractions.

FIBRES

The word "fibre" seems to have become the in thing

Taking a snack on the trail. A plastic drinks bag containing a sweet drink or "fruit soup" is providing this backpacker with both liquid and carbohydrates.

(Opposite) Use this calorie table when planning your menu. You need in excess of 5,000 calories per day when backpacking.

at present, although it has been around for long enough. The importance of fibre in the diet is obvious to anyone who has spent an extended backpacking trip relying mostly on dehydrated food. Fibre comes mainly from vegetable sources and is mostly indigestible. That means that the molecules of baked beans, for example, are too large to pass into the gut, so we can enjoy them, feel full up with them lying in our stomach, and feel smug that we are not going to add extra calories because they will be passed through the system. Modern diets, especially those based on dehydrated and freeze-dried foods, can cause constipation on extended trips. It can also aggravate haemorrhoids, which may not be a pleasant subject but is one which afflicts many climbers who have spent too long

sitting on cold rocks. There is little doubt that roughage in the diet does ease disposal of waste.

LIQUID

The final element in our diet is our liquid intake. Physical exertions over a day's working can knock off some weight, remove valuable minerals, and leave one vulnerable to a number of problems. It is vital to replace liquid loss as soon as possible. A little, not too much, salt in the water can be a good thing, or you can now buy sachets containing replacement vitamins and minerals. If you are in a cold environment, a hot drink is necessary to raise body temperature, especially if the body is drained of energy and unable to keep itself warm.

Each of the above constituents has its place in our

CALORIFIC VALUES TABLE

	per hectogram (100 g)	per oz		per hectogram (100 g)	per oz
Apple	53	15	Ice cream	212	60
Apricots, dried	176	50	Lentils	88	25
Bacon, fried	441	125	Margarine	793	225
Bananas, fresh	70	20	Marmalade	264	75
Baked beans	92	26	Mars bar	458	130
Beef, corned	229	65	Milk, fresh	35	10
Beefburger	280	80	Milk, powder	353	100
Drinking chocolate	405	115	Orange, fresh	35	10
Cocoa	458	130	Peach, dried	212	60
Coffee, black	nil	nil	Peanuts, salted	564	160
Biscuits	420–530	120–150	Pear, fresh	35	10
Brazil nuts	635	180	Peppermints	388	110
Bread	247	70	Pie, chicken	282	80
Butter	793	225	Pie, steak & kidney	282	80
Cereals	317–353	90–100	Pineapple, tinned	70	20
Cheese, Cheddar	405	115	Porridge	53	15
Cheese, cottage	106	30	Potatoes, boiled	88	25
Cheese, cream	811	230	Potatoes, instant	335	95
Cheese, Edam	300	85	Prunes, dried	70	20
Cheese spread	282	80	Raisins	247	70
Chocolate	530+	150+	Rice, boiled	123	35
Cooking fat	882	250	Risotto, beef	123	35
Cream, fresh	212	60	Salmon, tinned	141	40
Crisps	530	150	Sardines, tinned	300	85
Egg, boiled	159	45	Sausages, beef	282	80
Egg, fried	247	70	Sausages, pork	335	95
Egg, omelette	194	55	Soups	18–70	5–20
Fish, dried cod	176	50	Soya flour	441	125
Fish, grilled	176–317	50–90	Spaghetti	370	105
Flour	353	100	Sugar, white/brown	388	110
Fruit squash	141	40	Sultanas	264	75
Glucose	388	110	Tangerines, fresh	35	10
Ham, boiled	212	60	Tea, black	nil	nil
Hazel nuts	388	110	Toffees	441	125
Honey	282	80	Walnuts	635	180

diet and it is easier now to see why a balanced intake of food is essential. We need the carbohydrates and fats to provide energy, and fuel and proteins to keep the body in good repair.

As we said earlier, the average adult male needs about 1,000 calories a day just to tick over, and about 3,000 calories a day to go about his daily work, providing he does not have a very physical manual job. But, as backpackers, we need in excess of 5,000 calories a day for such work as a 20-mile (32 km) walk on rough terrain with a 30-lb (14 kg) pack on our shoulders. If we try to eat massive meals at breakfast and lunch, there are still likely to be times when our sugar levels run low and boosters may be needed. But, as we have seen, this can lead to hypoglycaemia. So it may be better to eat less but more often, so that we can keep our sugar levels up without having to draw on fat reserves, thus reducing our efficiency. The harder we push ourselves, the greater is the need for energy. It is an area which has attracted very little official research, but Wander of Switzerland have come up with some interesting figures which show that a runner covering 10.8 ft (3.3 m) a second needs 4.9 calories per pound (10.8 calories per kilo) of weight each hour, while a sprinter covering 21.6 ft (6.6 m) a second requires 38.6 calories per pound (85 calories per kilo) of weight each hour—so, twice as fast yet requiring almost nine times more energy. From this sort of research the company has worked out that for speed sports such as cycle trials, a rider needs between 3,500 and 5,500 calories a day; for strength sports, the intake is about 4,500 and 8,000 calories; and for endurance activities between 4,000 and 7,000 calories. These figures are obviously guides, because every individual has different requirements according to age, sex, weight, and so on. We also have different metabolisms and that affects how we burn up energy. As a backpacker, it is fairly safe to suggest that you will need a minimum of 5,000 calories a day.

The Sierra Club in the United States has worked out that you need 2½ times as many calories to gain 1000 ft (305 m) of elevation as you do to walk at sea level for one hour at 2 mph (3.2 km/h). The United Nations Food and Agriculture Organization has suggested a 5% increase in calorie intake during winter provided we wear suitable clothing to keep body heat in.

One of the great dangers is that in our anxiety to ensure we have enough energy we actually overeat on the trail. And, anything that we cannot burn off as energy, gets stored away as fat. That may be the reason some backpackers actually put on weight in the course of a trip.

Having tried to understand what food we need, we should try to arrange our diet accordingly. Most outdoor food manufacturers, now conscious of the nutritional needs of their customers, do give this information on their products' packaging. But beware, most freeze-dried and dehydrated meals tend to be low on calories, averaging out at roughly about 400 calories. It is, therefore, easy to see that the daily diet has to be boosted considerably above these meals to reach the target intakes, especially if you are packing in winter and you need well in excess of 5,000 calories. But it is in the "padding out" of calories where the care has to be exercised. Dried potato is rich in carbohydrate, so a helping would add about another 360 calories to your freeze-dried meal. You may have enjoyed a sweetened cup of tea to begin with and a bar of chocolate or some cheese to finish, so your intake has risen to 1,300 calories or so. That may only be a third of your total daily requirement.

Nuts are useful to nibble along the trail but are about 90% fat, and unless you are going to burn off the energy, you are simply going to put on weight. But, having said that, nuts are a rich source of energy. Peanuts have 170 calories per ounce, brazil nuts 180 calories, and walnuts 150.

So, if we are going to satisfy our daily nutritional requirements, it is necessary to work out a balanced feeding programme. If you are away on a long trip, away from built-up areas, you are going to have to rely heavily on lightweight, dehydrated foods, the sort of things we have been using for years without appreciating it.

Many companies are now offering freeze-dried and dehydrated meals, most of which can be cooked by simply adding water, stirring, and allowing to reconstitute. These meals generally form the basis of our menu planning. Around this meal base you must have other sources of energy, i.e. calorie-packed food. Apart from the obvious, such as granola (muesli) bars, chocolate, and so on, there are newer products now available which supply all the important nutrients the body requires in drink form. Available in various flavours, a packet can act as a meal substitute, if necessary, and has the advantage that it can be taken simply by adding some water.

It is amazing how long wholemeal bread will keep. I have known it to remain fairly edible for a week or so, provided it is kept in an air-tight container.

Everyone should try to discover their own basic metabolic rate. You will already know if you tend to put on weight or take it off during a trip. If you take it off, you are either overweight or your diet was not calorie-loaded enough. If you put weight on, you just eat too much.

Camp chores

With your kitchen organized, you can either cook supper, or else get rid of the various chores and enjoy supper later. Washing socks and shirts is one of the regular chores of extended backpacking trips. Clean feet and socks are a must if you are to avoid discomfort and blisters. Many backpackers change socks at lunchtime and, if possible, wash them then, so that there will be plenty of time for them to dry out before they are needed again. Others prefer to wait until camp has been pitched, before getting down to this necessary chore. I rarely let my socks get really dirty. The advantage of this is that all you have to do is freshen them up by a quick scrub in cold water, and then allow them to dry. If the sun is hot, then they will dry very quickly if laid out on top of the tent. If the weather is not so good, you will have to dry them inside the tent, by hanging them over the stove as you cook supper, or by hanging them over the candle or lantern. Underwear and shirts are the other items which will need washing at fairly regular intervals, although, again, there are those who do not bother. I tend to walk on, allowing my clothes to become smellier and smellier until I can say for sure that I will be able to dry them. If the weather is continuously bad, I will smell continuously bad, but as soon as the sun shines through, and there appears to be a drying breeze, I will have a washing day. My attitude is simple. I would rather wear smelly clothes than wet ones.

Washing clothes in the evening is not always the best time for this chore. If the sky is clear there is every possibility that there will be a heavy dew or frost, so it is pointless leaving clothes outside in such conditions. Do the washing in the morning in these situations, and tie the clothes to the outside of your pack, so that as you walk along, the sun will dry them.

CAMP EVENINGS
Most backpacking camp evenings are spent in idle chat, or, if solo, in luxuriant laziness. Some backpackers may enjoy a game of cards, dice, or do a crossword puzzle. My regular activity is to catch up on my reading. A good book is a good friend,

Hygiene is important when on the trail, and it is especially important to have clean socks. Many backpackers wash their socks in the morning and hang them on their pack with pegs. By evening, or by lunchtime if the sun is hot, the socks are dry.

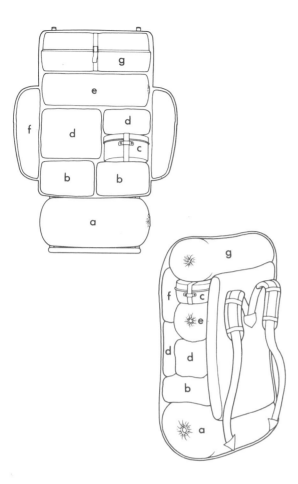

(Opposite) Morning chores in wild surroundings. Sleeping-bags and clothing are turned inside out, shaken out and aired.

Packing the rucksack, ready for the day's hiking: **(above)** a framed pack, **(below)** a frameless. *(a)* Sleeping-bag. *(b)* Change of clothes. *(c)* Cook-set. *(d)* Camp food. *(e)* Tent.

(f) Water bottle. *(g)* Insulation mat. In the pockets, snacks and camera—and separately, the fuel bottle. Maps go in the top-flap pocket.

(Above) A walking staff or a branch of a tree does a good job of propping up the rucksack, so that it can be easily packed.

and I rarely get the chance for light reading at home. In a group, there is the opportunity for exchanging books when you have read them, and if your travels take you through areas where there are mountain huts or hostels, you will invariably find a paperback book there for swapping. Evenings can also be spent planning the rest of the route, working out bearings in advance and making notes of them to save time later. If I pitch camp high on a mountain, I like to work out my exact position on the map and mark it before I turn in for the night. I also work out the bearings for my head-off direction in the morning. This not only saves time in the morning, but gives

me accurate positions in the event of low cloud or mist, so common in the mountains in the early morning, obscuring the view.

Eventually, it is time to turn in. One of the most marvellous sights in the backpacking game is to see a group of small tents, illuminated against the blackness of the night by flickering candle flame. Inside each tent, the occupants are snug, warm, and comfortable, insulated from the black of the night and the unknown of the wilderness. Over the years, I have used a variety of lanterns and flashlights, but it takes a lot to beat the humble candle. I like to take a hot drink to bed, and enjoy a light supper of chocolate, or cocoa. Occasionally I will douse the candle early, allow the blackness to infiltrate, and just enjoy being part of the wilderness night.

Once I am ensconced in my sleeping-bag there is very little, short of an emergency situation, which will make me get out of it until morning. But when "nature calls" you should always walk a good distance from camp. If possible, dig your latrine with a stick of wood or a small stone. Before breaking camp, make sure you cover everything up. Bury it as deep as you can, and don't just roll a rock on top of it. Bury the toilet paper too, or better still, burn it.

BREAKING CAMP

After breakfast, the time comes to pack up camp. Get your sleeping-bag out and air it as you work away at the morning chores. If the flysheet of your tent is wet with condensation, try and dry it off before you pack it up. If that is not possible, take it from your pack at the first opportunity in the course of the day, and allow the sun and wind to dry it out. There is nothing worse than erecting a wet tent at the end of the day.

Once you are packed, take a careful look around the camp site and make sure you are leaving it as though you had never been there at all. Leave absolutely no traces of your passing. If you have moved rocks or boulders for any reason, roll them back into their indentations in the ground, otherwise you will merely create new ones and in no time at all the ground will be covered in a series of pock marks. Take every bit of litter with you, even matchsticks. Remember: if you pack it in, pack it out. This is vital to the future of our environment. Don't allow it to become run down, remember this is the only planet we have. We must take care of it not only for ourselves, but for our children, and for their children.

CAMPING PROBLEMS

Finally, let us take a look at some problems that may arise in the course of our camping stopover.

Biting insects, such as mosquitos, blackflies,
"no-see-ums", and gnats can turn the most beautiful of camps into a living hell. Insect repellants do work, and it is a good idea to spray your head, around the collar of your shirt, around the cuffs of your shirt, and around the bottoms of your trouser legs. Spray some onto your hands and wipe it over all exposed skin, being careful not to wipe it into your eyes or onto your lips. The best tents have mosquito netting, but if yours does not, spray the entrance of the tent with repellant. Mosquito coils, internationally branded as Tiger Rings, smoulder away without a flame, and work very well. My preference, inside the tent, is to smoke a pipe. This does not always endear me to those who share my tent, but it does keep insects out.

Damp clothing can also be a problem. No matter what the weather is like, by the time you have walked a few miles with your pack on, your inner clothes at least will be damp from perspiration. As soon as you settle in for the night, strip off, put on some warm dry clothing, and put your damp clothes out to dry, or, if it is damp outside, put them inside a stuff sack. Some campers recommend jumping into the sleeping-bag while still wearing the damp clothes, believing that the dampness will evaporate in the warmth of the bag. I have never found this to be the case, and all that happens is that you dampen your sleeping-bag, which is something to be avoided at all costs. Always keep the inside of the tent as dry as possible. It may be an unpleasant thought, but once you have put your damp clothes on in the morning, they will very quickly dry out.

It is always a good idea to use a lighter for backpacking trips as, unlike matches, they do not suffer from dampness. Having said that, in my experience, lighters always seem to pack up when I need them most. A spare lighter is the answer, or a good supply of matches wrapped in a waterproof container. Keep some in your food bag all the time, or along with your emergency rations. When you are actually cooking, tuck the box of matches or your lighter inside your sleeping-bag, where it will stay dry, or in your shirt pocket where you will find it easily.

Chap. 7

BACKPACK-ING TRAILS

To the city-bound, it seems incomprehensible that this tight little country of ours can offer a variety of long-distance walking routes perhaps without equal in the world. Scenic variety is the delight of the United Kingdom, where every whim and fancy can be catered for without overlong journeying to the start of the chosen trail. Any point within the boundaries of these islands can be reached in a day or so of travelling, whether the traveller lives in the far north of Scotland, or in southernmost Cornwall, and an admirable network of public-service transport can, with a little forethought and planning on our part, allow us to penetrate into the most remote of corners to pick up, or leave, a trailhead of our choice.

And what a choice we have. There is, for the purist, wilderness aplenty, and I do not mean the wilderness of the overused trite phrase. I mean wilderness as defined by international conservation bodies, who, in the past several years, have realized the importance of such areas for the scientific study of land which has not suffered from man's interference. Areas of wild uncompromising wilderness which, by its own accord, has rebuffed attempts by man to fertilize the ruggedness and sterility of its coastline, hills, and mountains. Areas where man has tried in vain to wrestle a living from the stark landscape. Areas of wild land, labelled by the unfeeling layman as bleak, windswept, arid, and even worthless, but land which nevertheless lifts the hearts and quickens the pulse of those who care and love such places.

In contrast, but equally loved by many, is the gentle English landscape so revered and praised in art, poetry, and song, the lands of gentle pastures, hedgerows, and stone dykes. Who can fail to be captivated by the appeal of the English country pub at the end of a day's walk; who can fail to be sentimentally struck by the twinkling lights and welcoming glow of a twilight lakeland village as one leaves the falls at the end of a winter's walk; who can fail to experience the affinity with the hospitable folk of the Yorkshire Dales, or enjoy a brief chat with an upland shepherd? The country lanes of Dorset, Norfolk, and Devon are not wilderness but have an attraction of their own, an attraction that brings to mind the older quieter days when life was lived at a smoother pace. Take too to the coastline, where the oceans pulse steadily and often dramatically against steep cliffs, cruel rocks, and wide silent beaches. Here you walk in company with the harsh call of gulls, you live with the heady wine of salt-tanged winds and you gaze constantly upon the anonymous horizon, a horizon which breeds and nurtures the coming weather, be it storm or calm. Spend a day, if you like, exploring the cobbled fascinations of an old fishing port, where white-washed cottages stand as a testament to the gnarled salt brines who live there, the folk who share a deep affinity with most backpackers, the folk who gain sustenance, and indeed their livelihood, from the great giver that is the ocean.

The coastline of Britain is rich in potential experience, from the historic Northumbrian castles and headlands to the salt flats of Essex, where the mists roll in as muffling waves turning a golden world into one of silent pewter. Go too to Ireland, to the west coast of Clare, where one walks in the company of ancient folk song, or to the magic Dingle peninsula where, it is said, on a clear day, you can see the skyscrapers of New York, the nearest neighbours. It was from a lonely creek in the shadow of Mount Brandon that St. Brendan "the fearless" set sail for North America, to conquer the perils of the Atlantic hundreds of years before Christopher Columbus. There is no finer way of learning history than by backpacking. Walk in the footsteps of your country's heroes and discover the land as they did. Explore Scotland's Trossachs in the steps of the Gregorach, the Children of the Mist, immortalized by the pen of Sir Walter Scott. Or walk from near Aviemore to Fort William on the line of the ancient Rathad nam Mearlach, the Rievers road, ancient byeways which still resound to the ghostly grunting of stolen cattle and the Gaelic cries of the rieving clansmen.

But enough of my favourites. The highways and byeways, the mountain tracks, and the trails are there for everyone to explore for themselves. No one can tire of them, for the scope is well without human grasp. Even the most experienced backpackers and walkers of my acquaintance, and that includes a handful of outdoor septuagenarians who have walked and camped all of their lives, have only a limited experience of what Britain has to offer.

In 1949, the National Parks and Access to the Countryside Act provided the legislation for the creation of the official long-distance footpath, a creation which today allows unhindered access to the best of English and Welsh countryside. The "official" footpaths have been based on a definite geographical or historical feature, with continuous rights-of-way throughout their length, whether that way be on footpaths, bridleways, tracks, or even stretches of road. Not content with the ten or so "official" long-distance footpaths, many local groups of enthusiasts have also created their own "ways", based on existing networks of rights-of-way.

But the long-distance footpath concept is something of an anomaly to generally accepted backpacking dogma. Many are loath to follow signposts for days on end and seek instead their own ways of wandering, but legally, this can often be difficult. Happily, access law in Scotland is more relaxed than in England or Wales, although the long-distance footpath bug has bitten that country too. Scotland has, at time of writing, one "official" footpath, the West Highland Way, a popular route from Glasgow to Fort William. Two more are in the "official" pipeline. Right-of-way paths criss-cross the upland areas of Scotland, and generally speaking, in the highlands, walkers can go where they please, provided that they respect the countryside and accept that during the deer-stalking and grouse-shooting season they should stay away from the areas where hunting is in progress. This is a small price to pay for the "gentlemen's agreement" between landowners and walkers which has been the way in Scotland for generations.

As this is primarily a "how-to" book, rather than a "where-to" book, I do not intend making a full list of all the possible backpacking routes in Britain. Full lists of footpaths and National Parks can be had from elsewhere (see bibliography), but for guidance, I have listed all the "official" long-distance "ways" and some of the unofficial ones. Bear in mind, though, that much pre-trip fun can be had by planning your own journey instead of merely deciding to follow signposts indiscriminately, not that the following of signposts on long-distance footpaths should be shunned. For legal reasons, signposted routes should be followed, and the inexperienced hiker will be wise to use them. But consider the marvellous heritage we have encased within the grid lines of our Ordnance Survey maps. Spread them out before you on a dark winter's night in front of a roaring fire, and plan, and dream. Backpacking fun begins long before your first tentative footstep…

The Cleveland Way

The Cleveland Way was the second long-distance footpath to be officially designated. It forms a 100-mile (160 km) horseshoe route which, for much of its length, follows the rim of the North York Moors National Park. Add to that a final section on the "cliff lands" of Cleveland, fine coastal walking, and you have a mixture of high moorland and coastal walking which shows much of the best of the north-east of England.

The route begins in the market town of Helmsley, and crosses the River Rye not far from the ruins of twelfth-century Rievaulx Abbey. Wooded valleys lead to Sutton Bank and the Hambleton Hills where you can gaze across the wide panorama of the Vale of York towards the distant Pennines. As you approach Osmotherley, remember the Bronze Age folk who once tramped these remote parts, and more recently, the cattle drovers from Scotland and Northumbria who travelled southwards to the great cattle trysts of the south-east. Just north of Osmotherley, the footpath joins the line of the Lyke Wake Walk, perhaps the most popular of all England's challenge walks, for 12 miles (20 km) or so, passing over the wild Cringle Moor, and past the giant Wainstones at Hasty Bank. Next comes the highest spot on the walk, 1,500 ft (460 metres) above the level of the sea at Botton Head. Above Kildale, there is a monument to Captain Cook at Easby Moor, before the path crosses Great Ayton Moor, Highcliff,

Guisborough and passes on towards the distant sea at Saltburn.

With the sound of one of the wildest coastal stretches in England now ringing in your ears, you pass over Boulby Cliff, the highest cliff in England, to the interesting fishing village of Staithes, and onto Runswick, Lythe Bank and Whitby. Roman legions once walked over these coastal paths. From Whitby, a small town well worth exploring, continue past the North Cheek of Robin Hood's Bay (a derivation of the Celtic word "raphen" meaning cliff, and nothing at all to do with the medieval hero), through Ravenscar and past Scarborough to finish just short of Filey. An unofficial coastal path carries you on into the town itself. The Cleveland Way is not a difficult walk, but parts of it are exposed and notoriously wet and windy. Accommodation is plentiful, including several youth hostels, for most of the route, but bear in mind that there is no accommodation available on the 25 miles (40 km) between Osmotherley and Guisborough. There are many good potential camp sites for the camper.

Youth Hostels
Boggle Hole, Helmsley, Saltburn, Scarborough, Westerdale, Wheeldale, and Whitby.

Maps
O.S. series 1:50,000. Sheet Numbers: 93, 94, 99, 100, 101. The Tourist Map of the North York Moors is a useful addition to carry along.

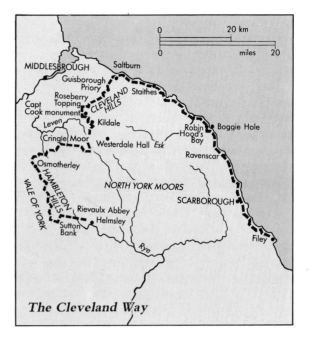

The Cleveland Way

Guidebooks
Cowley, W. *The Cleveland Way*. Dalesman Books, York, 1975.
Boyes, Malcom. *A Guide to the Cleveland Way*. Constable, London, 1977.
Falconer, A. *The Cleveland Way*. HMSO, London, 1972.
A Cleveland Way Information Sheet is available from the North York Moors National Park.

The North Downs Way

Running for 141 miles (225 km) from Farnham in Surrey to Dover in Kent, the North Downs Way is not the most popular long–distance footpath for backpacking campers, as camp sites are few and for much of the length of the walk, potable water is very scarce. However, it is a scenically attractive walk, passing as it does through the Kent Downs and the Surrey Hills. The wilderness value of the North Downs Way is nil, but as a training walk for backpackers from the London and South East area it is valuable. Consider that the Way passes over or under no less than eight main arterial roads, and at no time can you really escape from the fact that you are very close to civilization. Indeed, it is one of the most populous areas of Britain.

The real gems of this walk are the occasional copses of oak, beech, and ash, densely wooded and quiet, and in the stretches with ancient historical connections. One or two parts of the route trace the old Pilgrim's Way, and the route was in use over 2,000 years ago as one of the highways which converged onto Salisbury Plain and the Stone Circles at Stonehenge and Avebury.

The path starts at the railway station at Farnham (on the London Waterloo line), and follows the River Wey for a short distance before climbing to the north of Crooksbury Hill, past the villag of Seale and on towards Puttenham. Below the A3 Guildford Bypass, the path passes to the south of Guildford, where it joins the historic Pilgrim's ay to climb St. Martha's Hill, and on towards the .25 at Box Hill. Box Hill has literary associations with such worthies as Meredith and Keats, and as such is a popular picnicking place for day trippers. Stepping stones cross the River Mole before the short steep climb to Box Hill itself, from where the path runs across the chalk escarpment to Colley Hill, Reigate Hill and on past Gatton Park to the

A23, the Brighton Road. White Hill and Gravelly Hill take us to the A22, the Eastbourne Road, and on to Tatsfield in Kent, before climbing the scarp of the downs to Wrotham and the A20, the Hastings road.

More climbing over the escarpment, this time over Holly Hill towards the River Medway near Rochester. A footpath beside the M2 crosses the river by a footbridge and then the path turns south via Bluebell Hill to Detling, Thurnham Castle, and Hollingbourne to where it again joins up with the Pilgrim's Way to Boughton Aluph.

Leave Boughton Aluph and cross the downs towards Stowting, Castle Hill, and Sugarloaf Hill to the A620 just north of Folkstone. From a public house called the Valiant Sailor, there is a path over the cliffs to Dover, but, sadly, part of this area is used by the Ministry of Defence for target practice, so check that it is safe to cross before heading out. The end of the North Downs Way is at Shakespeare

Cliff, overlooking the wide waters of the English Channel. Give yourself a week for this walk, and be prepared for accommodation difficulties, especially in the summer months.

Youth Hostels
Tanners Hatch, Holmbury St. Mary, Crockham Hill, Doddington, Canterbury, Dover.

Maps
O.S. series 1:50,000. Sheets 178, 179, 186, 187, 188, 189.

Guidebooks
Wright, Christopher John. *A Guide to the Pilgrims Way and the North Downs Way.* Constable, London, 1971,
Dogget, T and T. *The North Downs Way.* Ramblers Association Booklet, 1978.

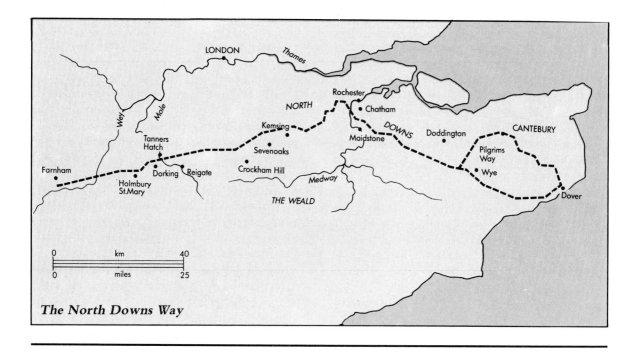

The North Downs Way

Offa's Dyke Path

It is a far cry from the downlands of Surrey and Kent to the wild border marches of Wales. For over a third of the total 168 miles (270 km) of Offa's Dyke Path, we follow the distinctive man-made earthwork that was built in the eight century by Offa, King of Mercia, as a frontier between England and

Wales. Offa's Dyke is a rugged walk, with plenty of uphill climbing and plenty of exposure to wind, rain, mists, and even blizzards... But it is beautiful countryside to explore, whether it be the Iron Age forts and castles, the interesting market towns, or the succession of bleak moors, deep valleys, mountain ridges, and tightly knit woodlands.

From the Severn Bridge the path takes you to

Chepstow and then climbs to Wintours Leap, a dramatic cliff with marvellous views. Follow the Wye, pass close to Tintern Abbey and so towards Monmouth, where the Wye and the Monnow are crossed. At Pandy, you start to climb up into the Black Mountains to a height of 2,000 ft (600 m), before dropping down to Hay-on-Wye. Gladestry, Kington, and Knighton are passed before you go through the Clun Forest to the Severn at Buttington. Follow the river now for a distance, and then pass through Llancynech to Bakers Hill, past Chirk Castle and across the valley of the Dee by the Pontcyscyllte aqueduct.

Now we follow the vale of Llangollen to Eglwyseg Mountain, and then across the moors to Llandegla where the River Alun must be crossed several times to reach the Clwydian Hills, a high ridge walk climbing to some 2,000 ft (600 m). The path continues through Bodfari and on to Prestatyn by Liverpool Bay.

Youth Hostels
Severn Bridge, St. Briavels Castle, Capel-y-ffin, Glascwm Clun Mill, Llangollen, Maeshafn.

Maps
O.S. series 1:50,000. Sheets 116, 117, 126, 136, 148, 161, 162.

Guidebooks
Noble, Frank. *The Shell Book of Offa's Dyke Path.* Queen Anne Press, London, 1972.
Wright, Christopher John. *A Guide to Offa's Dyke Path.* Constable, London, 1976.
Jones, J.B. *Offa's Dyke Path.* HMSO, London, 1976.
Roberts A. *Offa's Dyke Path.* Ramblers Association Booklet.
Richards, M. *Through Welsh Border Country Following Offa's Dyke Path.* Thornhill Press, Gloucester, 1977.

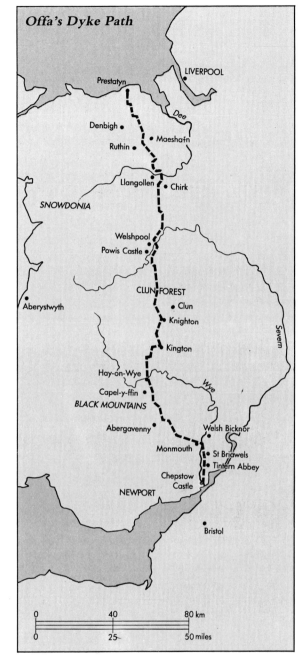

Offa's Dyke Path

The Pembrokeshire Coast Path

This footpath jealously hugs that part of the Welsh coastline which runs from Poppit Sands, near St. Dogmaels, to Amroth, on the Teifi estuary in the south. It is often a wild coastline, and lonely, even in peak holiday times, and in winter you can walk alone for days in the company of wheeling gulls,

cormorants, shags, guillemots, razorbills and oyster catchers, hundreds of them. Areas of the coastline hereabouts boast some of the oldest rock in the world (pre-Cambrian), and the entire walk shows samples of nature's superb handiwork, of the great awesome forces which have twisted and flattened, upthrust and folded the land masses on this edge of Wales. The sea, forever powerfully eroding its way inland, has helped shape the land too, and has formed coves, sea stacks, and caves, all which make

149

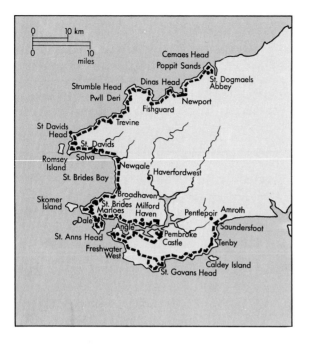
The Pembrokeshire Coast Path

this coastal walk constantly interesting and attractive. The Pembrokeshire Coast Path is 168 miles (270 km) long, and not unduly difficult. Accommodation is available for its entirety, but be careful in summer when hotels, guest houses, and even camp sites may be booked to overflowing. Only in a couple of places does the path actually leave the coastline, so a detailed route description is not really necessary.

Youth Hostels
Poppit Sands, Pwll Deri, Trevine, St. Davids Head, Pentlepoir.

Maps
O.S. series 1:50,000. Sheets 145, 157, 158.

Guidebooks
Barrett, J.H. *The Pembrokeshire Coast Path.* HMSO, London, 1974.
Miles, E.D. *Pembrokeshire Coast National Park.* HMSO, London.

The Pennine Way

The Pennine Way was the very first of the long-distance footpaths to be officially designated by the Countryside Commission expressly for those who "feel the call of the hills and the lonely places". It runs for a haughty 270 miles (435 km) up the backbone of England from Edale in Derbyshire to Kirk Yetholm just over the Scottish border. In theory, it is a marvellous walk, over the top of the Pennines in a wild corridor sandwiched on either side by industrial belts, for the most part well out of sight. There is much evidence of the industry of early times, too, in the old mine workings, drove roads, and numerous Roman roads, and the geological features at Malham, High Force, and Cauldron Snout are among the finest in Britain. Fine walk as it is, there is no walk in Britain so maligned and criticized by backpackers as the Pennine Way. Being the first official long-distance footpath, it was largely experimental, and many of the experiments have evidently failed. It is also a popular route, probably because it was the first and one of the longest, and as such suffers chronically from over-use. Large areas of boggy ground, long ribbons of wet eroded footpath and tales of woe regarding inexperienced backpackers have given the Pennine Way a bad press, but, despite the complaints, the Pennine Way remains the most popular of all the official footpaths and will probably remain so, for it is a logical route and offers the city-bound backpacker the solitude that he or she seeks. From Edale, the footpath climbs without further ado onto the Kinder Plateau, a bleak inhospitable morass of peat bog... Not all is misery, though, for on a good frosty winter's day, the fine waterfall of Kinder Downfall may be frozen, offering good sport to ice climbers. After the A57 at Snake Pass comes more Peak peat until a descent brings us to the Crowden reservoir and the A628 road. Another two roads have to be crossed before reaching Blackstone Edge and the beginnings of the well-loved Brontë country, passing en route the reputed site of Wuthering Heights on Haworth Moor. The walking now becomes easier and the Pennine Way backpackers can at last begin to shake down and lengthen stride. A beautiful walk along Airedale in the Yorkshire Dales National Park takes us to one of the "Ways" highlights at Malham Cove, a magnificent limestone cliff with a waterfall which was once larger than Niagara...

Beyond Malham Tarn, there are some long pulls onto Fountain Fells and then to Pen-y-Ghent. Descend to Horton-in-Ribblesdale, walk the beautiful trail to Hawes in Wensleydale, then past the superb waterfall of Hardraw Force to begin the long climb to Great Shunner Fell. Beyond Great Shunner Fell, descend to Thwaite, and then climb

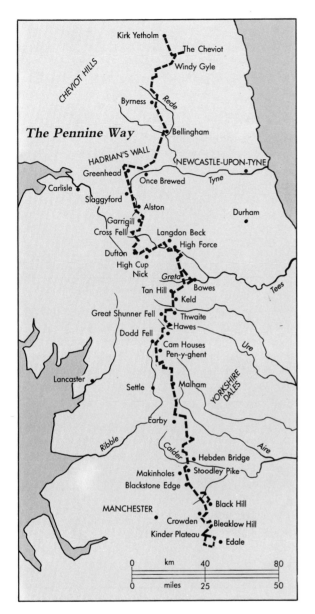

The Pennine Way

The highest point on the Pennine Way comes soon after Dufton, the 2,930-ft (893 m) summit of Cross Fell. There is a magnificent view from here, and on a clear day the Lake District peaks stand out plainly, as do the rolling hills of the Scottish Border. The valley of the South Tyne is followed now to Alston, Slaggyford, and Greenhead. We follow in the steps of the Romans now as the way takes the line of Hadrian's Wall, almost as far as Housesteads, one of the most interesting forts on the Wall. Beyond the Wall, forests dominate the line of the "Way" until the edge of the Cheviots are reached. Here begins the final and most difficult stretches of the walk. First, a steep climb takes you out of Redesdale to Coquetdal, and then you go on through extensive peat bogs and high moorlands, before the path begins to drop towards the destination of Kirk Yetholm, over the border into Scotland and the end of the Pennine Way.

The Pennine Way is a serious undertaking, and weather can decide whether the walk is a success or purgatory. Be well equipped and know how to use a map and compass competently.

Youth Hostels

Edale, Crowden, Mankinholes, Earby, Malham, Hawes, Keld, Dufton, Langdon Beck, Alston, Once Brewed, Bellingham, Byrness, Kirk Yetholm.

Maps

O.S. series 1:50,000. Sheets 74, 80, 86, 91, 92, 98, 103, 109, 110.

Guidebooks

Binns, Alan Penrose. *Walking the Pennine Way.* Gerard Publications, 1972.

Marriot, Mike. *The Shell Book of the Pennine Way.* Queen Anne Press, 1968.

Oldham, Kenneth. *The Penine Way: Britain's Longest Continuous Footpath.* Dalesman, 1972.

Stephenson, Tom. *The Pennine Way.* HMSO, London, 1969.

Wainwright, Alfred W. *A Pennine Way Companion.* Westmorland Gazette, 1968.

Wright, Christopher John. *A Guide to the Pennine Way.* Constable, 1975.

steadily up over Stonesdale Moor to Tan Hill, and the highest pub in England at 528 m (1,732 ft). Middleton in Teesdale is the next stop before following the River Tees past the famous waterfall at High Force, and the lesser known one at Cauldron Snout. Other spectacular scenic delights include the natural amphitheatre of High Nick Cup. The path then drops to Dufton and the Vale of Eden.

The Ridgeway

The Ridgeway has the reputation of being the easiest of all the long-distance footpaths, but camping is not generally recommended along it as there is a severe scarcity of water on the route. Beginning in Ivinghoe in Buckinghamshire, the Ridgeway runs for 85 miles (137 km) to near

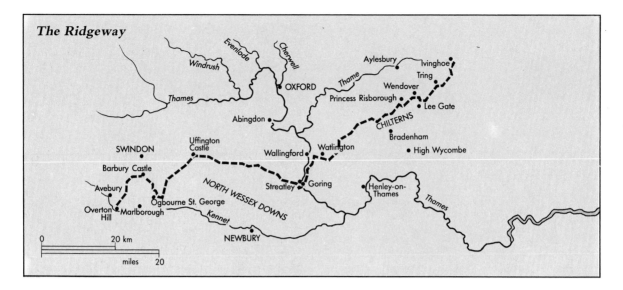

The Ridgeway

Avebury in Wiltshire, the first half of the walk using prehistoric pathways, and the second half being nearly all bridleway.

Leave the village of Ivinghoe and climb the 800-ft (244 m) Ivinghoe Beacon. Descend to cross the Tring Gap and then climb again for the high-level route to Wendover. From here, Coombe Hill is climbed, and then the path runs through magnificent extensive beechwoods, through the Chequers Estate, and then down to Princes Risborough. A short section on the road takes us to Lodge Hill, and then by following the foot of the scarp we pass below the M40 and walk just south of Watlington.

Some pleasant walking comes now, across Swyncome Down and through Ewelme Park before turning due west at Nuffield to follow Grim's Ditch, the ancient boundary, to Mongwell

and North Stoke and the River Thames. Follow the river to Goring and then take the road to Streatley.

We are now on the line of the ancient Great Ridgeway, which cross the Berkshire Downs before dropping down to West Overton near Avebury.

Youth Hostels
Ivinghoe, Lee Gate, Bradenham, Streatley.

Maps
OS series 1:50,000. Sheets 165, 173, 174, 175.

Guidebooks
Westacott, Hugh. *A Practical Guide to Walking the Ridgeway Path*. Footpath Publications, Adstock, 1977.

The South Downs Way

A 80-mile (129 km) bridle path, the South Downs Way wanders its way in between the Kent coast and Hampshires boundary with West Sussex. It begins in Eastbourne, and after climbing Willingdon Hill passes through Jevington to Alfriston. An alternative start for backpackers is at Beachy Head, and the route then crosses the Seven Sisters to re-connect with the bridle path at Alfriston.

From Alfriston, we climb the "whalebacks" of the Downs to Southease. Turning inland, we now by-pass Brighton by crossing the A27 and then the A23 near to Pyecombe, before climbing Devil's Dyke, Edburton Hill, and Truleigh Hill. Then the Way drops down into the Alder Valley.

Chanctonbury Ring, one of the highlights of the walk, is the next landmark of note, before we make our way to Amberley from where we have a series of hills to cross: Bury Hill, Bignor Hill, Burton Down, Woolavington Down, Graffham Down, and so to the A286 south of Cocking. We then have to cross Linch Down, Philliswood Down, and Beacon Hill before finishing at South Harting.

Youth Hostels
Beachy Head, Alfriston, Patcham, Truleigh Hill, Arundel.

Maps
O.S. series 1:50,000. Sheets 197, 198, 199.

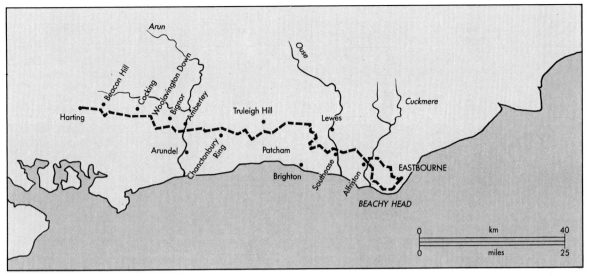

The South Downs Ways

Guidebooks
Teviot, CJ.K. *Walks along the South Downs Way.* Spurbooks, 1976.
Jennet, Sean. *South Downs Way.* HMSO, London, 1977.

Eastbourne Rambling Club. *Along the South Downs Way.* Available from 28, Kinfauns Ave., Eastbourne, East Sussex BN22 8SS.

The South West Peninsula Coast Path

From Minehead in Somerset to Poole harbour in Dorset, the South West Peninsula Coast Path is all of 515 miles (829 km) in length, faithfully following the coastline of Britain's south-western extremity.

It is, in fact, five long-distance footpaths made into one long continuous path. The sections are:
The Somerset and North Devon coast path, 82 miles (132 km).
The Cornwall north coast path, 135 miles (217 km).
The Cornwall south coast path, 133 miles (214 km).
The South Devon coast path, 146 miles (235 km).
The Dorset coast path, 76 miles (122 km).

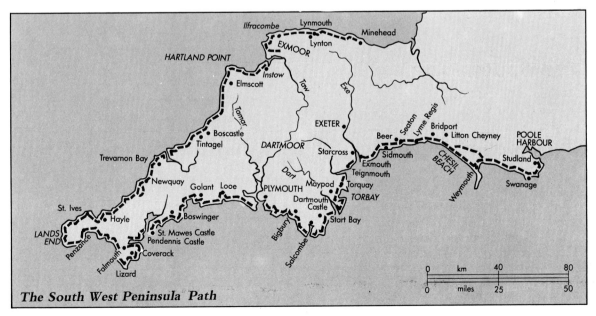

The South West Peninsula Path

Youth Hostels
Minehead, Lynton, Instow, Elmscott, Boscastle, Tintagel, Treyarnon Bay, Newquay, Hayle, Lands End, Penzance, Coverback Pendennis Castle, Boswinger, Golant, Plymouth, Bigbury, Salcombe, Start Bay, Maypool, Beer, Bridport, Litton Cheney, Swanage.

Maps
O.S. series 1:50,000. Sheets 180, 181, 190, 192, 193, 194, 195, 200, 201, 202, 203, 204.

Guidebooks
Marriott, Mike. *The Shell Book of the South West Peninsula Path.* Queen Anne Press, London, 1970.
Pyatt, Edward C. *The South West Coast Path*, David and Charles, Newton Abbot, 1971.
Southwest Way Association. *South West Way Footpath Information Sheet.* Beaver Lodge, Rundle Road, Newton Abbot, Devon.
Westacott, Hugh. This author has written a number of guide books to the individual sections of the South West Peninsula Path. Adstock Cottage, Adstock, Bucks.

Other long-distance footpaths in England and Wales

These are footpaths which, although not officially created by the Countryside Commission, exist due to the enthusiasm of local organizations. They include:

The Coast to Coast Walk: 190 miles (304 km) St. Bees Head, Cumbria to Robin Hoods Bay.

The Cotswold Way: 100 miles (161 km). Chipping Camden to Bath.

The Crosses Walk: 53 miles (85 km) across the North York Moors.

The Dales Way: 78 miles (125 km). Ilkley to Bowness on Windermere.

Hadrian's Wall: 75 miles (120 km).

Isle of Wight Coastal Path: 60 miles (96 km) around the island.

London Countryway: 205 miles (328 km) around London.

Lyke Wake Walk: 40 miles (64 km) across the North York Moors.

The Peakland Way: 96 miles (154 km) through the Peak District National Park.

The Staffordshire Way: 90 miles (144 km) from Mow Cop to Kinver Edge.

The Two Moors Way: 103 miles (165 km) crossing Dartmoor and Exmoor.

The Viking Way: 150 miles (240 km). Barton on Humber to Lincoln.

The Wolds Way: 67 miles (107 km) from North Ferriby to Filey. (Designated as an official long-distance footpath in 1982).

Yorkshire Dales Centurion Walk: 100 miles (161 km) . A circular route through the Yorkshire Dales National Park.

Long-distance walks in Scotland

At the time of writing there is only one long-distance footpath in Scotland, the West Highland Way which runs for 92 miles (147 km) from Glasgow to Fort William via Loch Lomondside, Glen Falloch, Tyndrum, Loch Tulla, Rannoch Moor, Kingshouse, Kinlochleven. Another two "official" paths, the Speyside Way and the Southern Uplands Way, are still in the planning process amid fierce objections from a growing conservationist lobby. The arguments against the "official" long-distance footpaths are basically that Scotland has different access laws than England and Wales, and people are free to walk more or less where they wish. By concentrating backpackers onto a thin ribbon of track, a signposted pedestrian motorway, erosion will take place and the immediate area of the track soon becomes a quagmire.

Even without "official" long-distance footpaths, Scotland is criss-crossed with rights-of-way, an excellent network which is looked after and documented by the Scottish Rights of Way Society. Their objects include the preservation and defence of public rights-of-way; the erection and restoration of bridges, sign posts, stiles, etc., and the defence and prosecution, directly and indirectly, of suits or actions for the preservation and recovery of rights-of-way. The Society can be contacted at 6 Abercromby Place, Edinburgh. Whilst access has rarely been challenged by landowners, the system can only work if walkers and backpackers avoid areas where deer-stalking and grouse-shooting are taking place. Highland estates, in particular, need the money that comes from sporting holidays, and an ill-placed backpacker can so easily disturb a shoot that has perhaps taken all day to stalk. Enquire locally where the shooting is taking place, and then avoid that area like the plague. In most areas, deer-stalking begins in early September, but officially from July 20th. It goes on until October 20th, although hind-culling goes on until February.

With the exception of certain marked areas, it is fairly easy to gain access during the hind cull. From August 12th grouse-shooting can affect low-level access. The golden rule to remember is: if in doubt, ask locally.

Bibliography

The New Complete Walker. Colin Fletcher. Alfred A. Knopf, New York. This book is, in my opinion, the finest treatise ever written on the arts of walking and backpacking. Should be on every backpacker's bookshelf if only for the sheer inspiration of the man's writing.

Backpacking: One Step at a Time. Harvey Manning. R.E.I., Seattle. A humorous look at backpacking written primarily for the beginner.

Backpacking in Britain. Robin Adshead. Oxford Illustrated Press, Yeovil. Now sadly out of print, this picture book captures the spirit of backpacking in the early seventies, and is a refreshing reminder of the simplicity of the sport.

Movin' On. Harry Roberts. Stone Wall Press, Boston. An excellent primer for the tyro winter walker. Chatty style, and full of sound common-sense advice.

Master Guide to Snow Camping. Cameron McNeish. Spurbooks. Well, if I don't plug it, no one else will. A snow camping guide for beginners.

The Walker's Handbook. Hugh Westacott. Penguin Books, London. A very useful reference book about walking. Excellent information on access laws and where to walk in Britain.

Walking Softly in the Wilderness. John Hart. Sierra Club Books, San Francisco. A very ecologically aware book. Should be read by every backpacker.

Mountaineering. the Freedom of the Hills. Edited by Ed Peters. The Mountaineers, Seattle. Primarily a how-to book about every facet of walking, climbing, and mountaineering.

Kit list

Before you go off on a backpacking trip, check everything as you pack it against a list of everything you are liable to need. There is nothing more frustrating than pitching your tent the first night out only to discover that you have left the tent pegs at home.

The following can be used as a guide.

Tent (including poles, pegs and spare pegs, guylines)
Sleeping-bag
Insulation mat
Stove
Fuel
Pots and pans
Mug
Spoon and knife
Matches or lighter
Candle
Flashlight
Water bag or water bottles
Food
First Aid kit
Map, compass, and altimeter
Towel and washing gear
Cloths for cleaning pots
Can opener
Spare clothes

INDEX